Back to Burma

for the love of John

Back to Burma
for the love of John

Mary Davey

London

Copyright © 1995 Mary Davey

ISBN 0 9526191 7 2

First published 1995 by
The Rathgar Press
Image House
Coombe Avenue
Croydon
Surrey CR0 5SD
England

No part of this publication may be reproduced by any means
without prior permission of the publishers.

A catalogue record for this book is available from the British Library.

Designed by David J Plumb ARCA PPSTD
Cover photograph: Andrew Bedingham
Archival photographic reproduction: Peter Mills Photography
Printed by Bakes & Lord Limited, Bradford

To my father

To Den

With love and thanks
for your contribution

10ter of August 1995

Contents

This book is a labour of love and determination, inspired by the men who were prisoners of war of the Japanese in World War Two. It is dedicated to all FEPOWs and their wonderful wives – the best friends I've ever had in my life.

It is written in loving and everlasting memory of Corporal John Edwin Davey, RAF Volunteer Reserve, 28th October 1916 – 27th December 1943.

Introduction

I nearly didn't publish this book. Thoughts of accusations of 'cashing in' on the Burma-Siam Railway fill me with abject horror. But what began as a simple tribute of love for a close member of my family, of whom I was so unjustly deprived, became so much more. It grew into a statement of empathy for all the men who lost their youth, innocence, sanity and lives. I found I had something to say, and God knows, not enough has ever or will ever be said on this episode of our history.

The Burma-Siam Railway is not a private nightmare. It is everybody's nightmare. That later generations do acknowledge, do care, do struggle to comprehend is perhaps the only pathetically inadequate gesture which ordinary people can make.

When I sought my father's permission to probe into the history of his brother, I was desperate to get his approval and support without upsetting him by raking over the past and all the painful memories it would invoke for him. I also questioned again and again my right to interfere into the lives and experiences of all the Far East Prisoners of War and to enter realms that were perhaps none of my business. My father gave me the kindest, most empathetic reassurance I could possibly have received. He replied softly, "Of course it's your business; he was your uncle".

Do I think this book is good? No, I'm a perfectionist and I always think I should have worked harder and achieved a better result, whatever I do. Besides which, I didn't write this because I wanted to produce a book or thought I was a writer.

Have I assumed some sort of mantle of knowledge and authority on my subject? No; I faithfully researched and worked hard in pursuit of a correct understanding of the facts, but they defy understanding. I may also have misinterpreted information or been misinformed or misled. I am undoubtedly also biased. Every effort has been made to be accurate, honest and balanced, to listen and to learn.

Many excellent books have been written by men who were prisoners of war of the Japanese and who worked on the Burma-Siam Railway. I cannot write as someone who was there, but only as the bewildered niece of someone who was there. John has helped me to write this account, but only in the most indirect manner. He didn't come home.

If I had been on that railway, I would be furious with the lack of attention the world has paid to my experiences. It would be of some little satisfaction to me to see others waking up to it albeit 50 years on. I am furious for my uncle that he was reduced to a casualty statistic of war and I want to give him life. This is the only way open to me; gently blowing on the flame of remembrance to give it power.

I had to write this book whether *I* wanted to or not. John wanted me to do this and now that I have, I hope that he is pleased and I pray that he is at peace.

Those valiant men who were there and who still survive, against all the odds; take pity on those who care more than they can ever say.

———————————

This book has developed naturally into three logical parts. Part 1, The Quest, describes the agonies of bereavement for an uncle I wasn't lucky enough to have. I believe that when you lose someone, eventually you find solace in your memories of them and the way they interacted with your life. When you didn't have them to start with, yet you still feel depths of love for someone who was your flesh and blood, it leaves you with an open-ended bereavement which is hard to cure.

Instead of sweeping aside John and burying his loss, I had to come to terms with it all; discover what he had gone through and confront it head on. I had to know *whom* it was that I mourned, and I also felt strongly that he had the right for his story to be told.

Peter Dunstan, an ex-Far East prisoner of war from the Thailand end of the line who devised and runs the Far East War Graves Archives calls this process 'laying ghosts to rest'. It is a very good description of the underlying instinct I have at times blindly followed in search of some satisfactory conclusion or outcome.

The chronological order of the search for information and its discovery and all the feelings of sorrow and joy, frustration and triumph were written on a virtual daily basis. The true picture emerges as the facts came to light.

Having plugged the gaps in John's story for which my father provided the outline and a lot of the filling, the second part of the book took shape, and even as I wrote it I saw something of my uncle taking tangible form at last. Had he died of natural causes at home, tragic though this would have been at so young an age, I think that my family would have found it easier to deal with. As it is, the circumstances of John's death will probably haunt us forever. As Weary Dunlop quotes in his war diaries, Major Corlette recorded upon the death of Pte E L Edwards who died of dysentery at Hintok Mountain on the 2nd June 1943, "This man was killed by the Nipponese just as surely as if he had been shot by them".

Yamaoka Michiko is a hibakusha (one who was exposed to the atomic bomb), in Hiroshima. She was hideously disfigured, and she did not have the kind of money necessary for plastic surgery. Her own people threw stones at her and called her 'monster'.

Haruko Taya Cook and Theodore F Cook interviewed her for their book, "Japan at War". She told them, "When I went to America I had a deep hatred toward America. I asked myself why they ended the war by a means which destroyed human beings. When I talked about how I suffered, I was often told, 'well, you attacked Pearl Harbour!' I didn't understand much English then, and it's probably just as well. From the American point of view, they dropped that bomb in order to end the war faster. But it's inexcusable to harm human beings in this way...". Yamaoka Michiko is absolutely, unequivocally right. It is inexcusable to harm human beings in *any* way.

———————————————

The inevitable ending to this book is The Pilgrimage. The culmination of all the work and the closest I can ever be to the man who was my Uncle John. In a way, this entire project was born out of the initial and persistent refusal I received to travel to a place which contains the physical remains of a member of my family, in order to honour him. That, to me, was the final insult and denial, and absolutely guaranteed my determination to succeed and carry out the mission.

It became more important, and more appropriate, to go to John as my efforts to do so gathered momentum, to the point where I simply couldn't rest until the journey was undertaken. I knew all along that I was asking for a 'ticket to the moon', and when I received one, it seemed all the more remarkable to me, rather than just another wrong put right.

I was quite aware of the untouched, unspoilt nature of Burma, which could equally be described as primitive; the suppressed people, despite their charming disposition, and the general Burmese nature of 'maybe, maybe not. The train might run, the plane might take off'. I also approached the pilgrimage with my eyes wide open, and I knew that all of the hurt and desperation would solidify for me in Thanbyuzayat. But nothing, nothing could have prepared me for the experience when it was ultimately fulfilled.

I'm incredibly lucky. I have a loving family and more moral support from my parents than is decent to ask for. I went to Thanbyuzayat to form a human bridge which my uncle could cross on his belated journey home. I took him my love, my respect and my heart.

Part I **The Quest**   5

As a very little girl I first became aware that my uncle had been killed at the hands of the Japanese during World War Two. I didn't understand.

John Edwin Davey was the younger brother, by 15 months, of my beloved dad, William Francis Davey, and my first thought was, if John was anything like my father he must have been terrific.

My second thought was that I had been deprived, along with my elder brother and sister of a very special uncle and perhaps an aunt and cousins. Our mother is an only child.

Over the years of my life I have come to love John very deeply and I sought, probably in my sub-conscious mind initially, to 'reconstruct' him, so that he would become a loving member of my close-knit, small family, as he would most certainly have done had he been allowed to live.

There isn't anyone alive who is loved more than John. He is revered by all of my family although only my father knew him personally out of those of us who survive today. Even my husband can be reduced to tears very easily at the remembrance of our loss and in particular, of course, the circumstances of that loss. I could never count my own tears.

In November 1991, the first time in my life that I had the resources to travel a long distance for what in no sense would be a holiday, I naively decided that I would visit John's grave, with the clear intention of 'bringing him home', spiritually, from his far-flung place of rest and back to the bosom of his family.

John is buried in Plot B6, Row J, Grave 11, Thanbyuzayat War Cemetery, Burma. I hit a brick wall with my very first, heartfelt request to visit my uncle. It had not occurred to me that anything could prevent the relatives and loved ones of servicemen from paying their respects to their dead, anywhere in the world.

Daveys are made of tough stuff, to the extent that John's death will trouble me to the end of my days because *he should have come home*. The Royal British Legion, a body for whom any sane individual must apply the highest regard, had said that permission to visit would not and has never been granted by the Burmese authorities. I could not accept this refusal.

In late 1988 I had started my own company from scratch and unknowingly entered a very difficult profession on the brink of severe economic decline. My Davey magic has brought me great successes in the face of adversity, but I had to concentrate all my efforts on my business to ensure its survival and I know that John would have supported my necessity to channel my energies on the job in hand. He was never far from my thoughts during this time.

My working life, since leaving school, has always involved marketing, and the power of publicity never ceases to amaze me. In July 1993 my husband handed me a copy of our local newspaper which contained a letter from Charles Peall, the Hon. National Public Relations Officer of the Burma Star Association.

Charles, who has become a dear friend and a constant source of inspiration, wrote, among other relevant things, of the significance of August 15th, the day of Liberation and I could not believe that firstly, here was a man who survived the Burma-Siam Railway and was still campaigning, and secondly, that Charles was local.

Without his kind help and interest I would not be in possession of all the information I hold today on John's story and the unbelievable experience of all the prisoners of war who were subjected to hell on earth. Through Charles I embarked on a wondrous voyage of discovery and realised that there is a huge network of associations and organisations run by groups of ex-POWs or individuals, some with funds, others on a shoestring and a few, by people like me, who were not directly involved in the hell but who care so much they want to do anything they can to carry forward the torch to future generations.

Somewhere along the line, John and I had a meeting of minds. He is incredulous at his fate and so am I. I owe it to this wonderful, grossly unfortunate man, who was my flesh and blood, to confront my fear of his ordeal and to humbly kneel before him and honour his memory and that of his many comrades. Before doing so, I had to find out as much as I could about what he had endured.

As was the case with so many survivors, men had the decency, the bravery and sheer kindness to write to the bereaved with important details and fond memories of their lost comrades. We were lucky enough to inherit a letter from one such great friend of John. He met John in Wiltshire when he was posted there by the RAF from Bridgnorth. They were both radio hams and John joined the RAF Volunteer Reserve as a radio mechanic.

John's additional documentation, such as it is, was retained by my grandfather, and is currently in my custody. Assorted photographs, many of John and my dad as little boys (terrors), some of a handsome young man in uniform, two letters home to his mum and dad, his birth certificate, a letter of condolence from George VI and four posthumously awarded medals. There are also letters from the Air Ministry and the Commonwealth War Graves Commission relating to his headstone. Not much to go on.

8

The next two logical steps were to push harder for permission to visit the cemetery in the right quarters, and to try and track down John's mate. The former action seemed comparatively easy. I wrote again to the Royal British Legion, to the Embassy of the Union of Myanmar requesting a visa and to the Foreign Office to complain that I had had no response to the latter. (In May 1989 the military government renamed Burma 'The Union of Myanmar'.) The second part seemed more difficult. I doubted the kind author of the letter would be at the address quoted in 1945. He wasn't listed in the telephone book for the entire area.

Charles Peall told me about Servicepals, the Teletext pages on Channel 4. I know that John and his friend were at RAF Seletar, Singapore at the time of the capitulation, from which they escaped by boat and managed to sink their vessel. With help from the Chinese they got to Sumatra where they were taken prisoner. My message detailing the vital points went out in September, together with a call for John's friend or anyone else who remembered him.

My three responses were very fruitful. A lady whose daughter went to school with John's mate's daughter rang to tell me that he'd hanged himself in 1966. This news intensified the anger I already felt at the treatment of the men, both as prisoners and survivors back at home. It also increased my fear of what they had been through.

The second call was from Sam Watson, whose father was killed in the Navy in World War Two and he has researched for years to piece together a picture of the dad he never knew. He gave me many tips on uncovering information and offered his friendship. Sam has visited the Chungkai Cemetery in Thailand and recommended that I contact Jack Cosford and acquire his book "Line of Lost Lives" and gave me Peter 'Tiny' Dunstans's telephone number (the founder of the Far East Prisoners of War Graves Archives), so that I could badger him for more details on John's grave and those of his fellow servicemen, searching for clues as to which camp he may have died in.

Sam shares my feelings on the crazy piece of history which was the Burma-Siam Railway and I'm encouraged to find another second generation 'campaigner'. There must be many others.

My third call was from Pam Stubbs, researching with her husband Les for the Imperial War Museum on RAF records, who suggested that with knowledge of many men captured in Sumatra they may find someone who knew my uncle. She asked me to send her all the information I had.

Through Charles I had contacted Harold Payne, through Jack Cosford I found Bill Holtham. Every contact gave me another contact. Magic was at work. I was on my trail at last.

Chapter 2

9

Everyone who reads this will know how little publicity has ever been given to the Burma-Siam Railway and the despicable treatment of prisoners of war meted out by the Japanese. I'd seen only one documentary on television and read one colour supplement article at this time and had only a sketchy grasp of the details as so little were given.

Some people enjoy learning about the horrors inflicted on others. I am not one of those people. I was frightened of finding out about things which would hurt me, but could not reconcile climbing metaphoric mountains to be able to embrace my uncle's grave, only to arrive there with the vaguest notion of his suffering. In any case, although sadness at his loss will never leave me, through a proper understanding of the circumstances I felt I might be able to come to terms with it.

Jack Cosford's wonderful book went a long way towards shedding light on areas of darkness. I could not put it down and read it cover to cover the day that I received it. It had an incredible effect upon me and began for me the process of putting the story into perspective.

The strength of character which brought this particular prisoner of war safely home was in evidence on every page of his book. Conditions which struck me as horrendous at the beginning became Jack's world for three and a half years, acquiring a curious acceptability as the book went on, through the author's own endurance. I began to understand that the nightmare was in essence an exercise in survival. I also became reluctantly aware that the further north men worked the worse conditions became, but later discovered that the coastal plains of Burma, beyond which John did not go, were considered 'preferable' when compared to the mountainous territory which separates Burma from Thailand.

The lessons which came out of "Line of Lost Lives" for me were that the worst deprivation can be fought with strength, resolve and acceptance without weakness. I will never understand how so many men did survive and there is glory in this testimony to the abilities of mankind. I was humbled to the point that I felt guilty that I wasn't out there and began to question my right to interfere into the lives and memories of men who shared an extraordinary bond; one they could only share by having been through hell and back together. I didn't feel at all worthy but I changed some of my values overnight. Material ones in particular.

Perhaps my reaction is a possible explanation for some other people being apparently disinterested or uncaring about what went on, but I knew that I had to continue with my quest, not only for John, but now for all the men who shared his fate and never came home and all the men who returned to face another battle – 'normal' life.

Thanbyuzayat War Cemetery is beautifully maintained by locally commissioned staff of the Commonwealth War Graves Commission. I have photographs to prove it. Every November, I believed, the Commonwealth Embassy Officials make a visit of remembrance there. Peter Dunstan made the trip to Thanbyuzayat in 1986, concurrently with the Embassy visit through the British Ambassador to Rangoon, and with his advice I applied for permission to do likewise in 1994.

This could be the only way that permission will be obtained unless the political situation in Burma changes. The cemetery is near to the Thai border and so are the resident Burmese freedom fighters. There are land mines in close proximity and according to Peter, the train he arrived on didn't wait long in the station because they tended to get blown up if they hung around. The area (though not the people) was inhospitable, poorly served by transport and totally devoid of accommodation or edible food, *at the time of his visit*. I still can't wait to get there!

Other people have made the trip before me but not many other British bereaved as far as I am aware. No one seems to want the responsibility for foreign visitors getting sick, getting lost or getting killed whilst on a pilgrimage. The Burmese have also cut themselves off from the rest of the world and are not renowned for their tourist industry. There are, however, ways and means to get around these barriers, quietly and persistently, or no civilians would ever have made it. I embarked on them all.

My letter from Pam Stubbs (researching for the Imperial War Museum) was amazing. Her principal source of information on John was due to the dedication and vigilance of both Dudley Apthorp, the Senior Officer of the Sumatra Battalion and Bob Grafton who co-ordinated records of the men from all three services (about 500) who escaped to Sumatra, including John Davey. These valuable records were published by Ann Apthorp, Dudley's widow, aided and abetted by Bob Grafton and Dot Grafton. For every wonderful exFEPOW there is, more often than not, a wonderful Mrs exFEPOW. Bob died from cancer two months after this valuable record went into print.

I of course bought a copy immediately of "The British Sumatra Battalion", and to see John's name in the nominal roll in the book made me prouder of him than ever. It also provided considerable comfort to know that the men were 'tracked' as far as was possible at the time.

In fact the 500 men of the British Sumatra Battalion stayed together until losses were inevitably incurred, and until July 1943, after which the sick were sent to Khonkhan (the 55km 'hospital camp') which began to split up the men. John was one of 20 from the Battalion sent to Khonkhan who died there. The camp's own version of Weary Dunlop, (the medical hero from the Thailand end of the line) was super-surgeon Colonel Sir Albert Coates, AIF.

Despite having a reasonable grasp as an outsider of the appallingly primitive and sparse comforts and facilities afforded to any of the men in any of the camps, it was helpful to me to know that there were dedicated and skillful MOs available who, though called upon to perform miracles, certainly achieved great feats against all the odds. Many men survived against these odds and although it was doubtless due to their own determination, they must have been greatly assisted by these brilliant medical men.

To know that John and all his comrades benefited from the discipline and structure of the unity of a battalion, no matter that its authority was enforced upon them, gave me great hope that John simply died because he became desperately ill and not because he was subjected to worse disorder, particularly ill treatment, cruelty or neglect. If his odds were as good or perhaps even better than the average, then the chances of his survival, had the dice been tossed in a different order, were not necessarily increased.

Dudley Apthorp was both cursed and adored by his 'adopted' men. A cross between Lawrence of Arabia and Leslie Howard in appearance, he frequently took beatings in defence of his men, protected his sick and improved conditions wherever possible.

Major L J Robertson, AIF, said of him, "Captain Apthorp's Battalion (POW) comprised a vast collection of men scattered from all three services and units; an assembly most unlikely to develop an esprit-de-corps. Yet, in fact, this is just what they did. They did set up a special unit feeling, as good as any old established regiment, that speaks so much for the leadership of Captain Apthorp."

Perhaps it was even better put by one of his men, CPO Jan Tucker, who said in a letter to his commanding officer, "Your great courage and determination to maintain discipline were responsible for us being alive, so thank you sir."

I was concerned that John should have been apart from his 'unit', other than his fellow victims, at Khonkhan. Who was holding John's hand when he died? I didn't know.

How can you love someone that you never had the good fortune to meet? I worship my father, and his brother John was loved by my father very much. John was different to my dad. Dad's tall and extremely lean; John packed a punch. He was brilliant at competitive sports and my Dad lost to John on frequent occasions – graciously – through gritted teeth. Their mum wrote to John when he was in Singapore to tell him, among many other things, that his older brother had won a darts championship. John replied that either his darts had improved considerably since he had last played him or he must have won in a very small village.

John wasn't terribly interested in the particular girls who took a great shine to him before he joined up at 24. He preferred radios at the time. Yet his considerable artistic talents extended to a superb pencil drawing of a rather beautiful young lady which still survives. My dad's surviving drawing is of a horse's head, not quite so pretty.

My dad has a great sense of humour. John was more laid-back and devil may care. But in photographs where they were almost always together, my dad's arm is so fondly and protectively placed around his brother, I see the bond which existed between them. That it was broken so cruelly and pointlessly and so early, my dad has had to live with all of his life, and so have I.

My elder brother was born in the year that John died and so he had an uncle for six months, and John had a nephew, though neither of them knew it. I envy him, all the same. My mother has described to me how much she and my father longed for John to come home and commented that the course of all our lives has been affected by his inability to do so. She never got to meet her brother-in-law.

My father rarely talked about John because it was obviously painful for him to do so, concerned, as he naturally was, about what his brother had suffered. Nevertheless my goal was to establish the truth and I could only hope that this may be better, in John's case, than the nightmares which haunt us. I wanted to bring us all some peace.

It is easy, fanciful and egotistical for me to imagine that John has somehow selected me to tread in his path and unveil the truth about his diabolical ordeal and premature death. Nevertheless I am driven in this quest. As if I was not already involved enough to demand answers and reasons on behalf of my own chromosomes, genes and DNA which lie in a far-flung part of Burma, I feel I have an additional force behind me which drives me on relentlessly.

There is more mystery in heaven and earth than mere mortals can ever understand, and perhaps I have become an instrument to play the most poignant tune and to answer unanswered questions and to finish unfinished business. I didn't understand what immortality was until I began to correspond at length on the subject of John Davey and his short life. The file is a ton weight, and his name lives on. He is worthy of so much more.

Very little attention is devoted here to the fight I have embarked upon to visit his grave. There's a very good reason for this. It is impossible to research into the building of the Burma-Siam railway without being irreversibly inspired by the guts and cast-iron resolve of the men whose story it is. I can't let a little thing like a brutal, military regime stand in my way, or I'd be showing myself up in the presence of unmitigated heroes. I will get there.

Once or twice, alone with my anger at John's fate, I did consider just trying to book a flight and attempt an illegal border crossing and to hell with the consequences. I'm afraid I'm not brave enough to have seen it through. It would have done no favours to my family to see me hurl myself on the funeral pyre.

It simply hasn't occurred to me that I'm not going to be allowed to go. As of Remembrance Sunday 1993 I have had no reply from the British Ambassador to Rangoon to my letter dated 21 October. No news is good news.

"I know that I'm a hostage to all his hopes and fears, I just wish I could have told him – in the living years."
Mike & the Mechanics 1988

Peter "Tiny" Dunstan (6' 6") was a terrific example of perseverance to me, since he survived the Thailand end of the railway and he's been to Thanbyuzayat! Peter spends a lot of time researching into the graves of men who were not transferred to the three cemeteries (Thanbyuzayat, Kanchanaburi and Chungkai), and has provided impossible information to the comfort of many a war widow - and niece. Peter established John's death camp from detailed maps of the line before the Sumatra Battalion was even known to me. I had the great pleasure to meet him and his wife, Lily, on 16th of November, 1993.

An incredible man, captured as a baby at 19, whenever I think about him it is with a smile at his humour and a picture of him researching the greatest wealth of documentation on any subject I have ever seen amassed outside a museum. He also, of course, has painstakingly filed on computer the records of the occupants of the war cemeteries.

I took with me a few bits and pieces of documentation which I thought might interest him. He had the original source material in full, which yielded the bits and pieces in the first place.

I hadn't realised what a major part Peter would play in the compilation of John's story until I met him, and understood the gaps of knowledge he has been called upon to fill for numerous relatives around the world and has succeeded in doing so.

Both Peter and Charles Peall have asked for John's RAF unit. I don't have this information, and no official records contain this detail either. Believe me, if Peter Dunstan doesn't already have this information on computer, it is very difficult to obtain!

Pam Stubbs to the rescue! In her research for the Imperial War Museum on RAF FEPOWs, Pam has unearthed a document issued by Squadron Leader Toby Carter. John was one of the RAF men based at the Air Ministry Experimental Station at Tanah Merah Besar, near Changi, a radar operation. Needless to say, the beloved FEPOW network comes into its own yet again through someone Peter happens to know, who might just be able to shed a little more light on further details.

I also heard from my dear friend Sam today, my fellow second generation campaigner. He is urging me to spread the information-seeking net into RAF circles, which cannot possibly do any harm. I was only temporarily deterred from this course of action knowing how split up the men became, and that John could have (please, God) died in the arms of someone that perhaps no official services' record could throw any light upon. I don't think it would have been very relevant what unit you were in when you were dying in the 55km camp, and whether anyone who was there for you was in the Army, Navy, RAF, a civilian, a native or a martian.

The structure which did exist and which perpetrated accurate records is of extreme importance, and without such information my efforts to date would have been useless. On Sam's sound advice, I wrote immediately to the RAF Records Department, RAF Insworth, Gloucester.

Peter gave me another gift on yet the same day. He told me that I am a member of the FEPOW family, and this gave me intense pleasure and a feeling of belonging and security, which nothing else in life can hope to equal. I began to realise that I have more uncles – and aunts – than anyone else could possibly have. I also feel that my own uncle is present in my life in a way that he couldn't be before.

There has been confusion over the precise date of John's death since my grandfather first informed the Air Ministry that they had incorrectly recorded this in 1952, the year of my birth; the year in which John's permanent headstone was finally placed in position. Unfortunately my grandfather didn't record his correspondence, and the Air Ministry didn't quote any dates in their letter telling him they'd noted their error and would correct it!

I have two dates. All official records – 17 December 1943. The 'British Sumatra Battalion' record – 27 December 1943. The Commonwealth War Graves Commission are still quoting the former date. Peter thinks Dudley Apthorp's records would have been correct. I agree. This was the source material of the 'official record'. Mistakes were made in the endless permanent recording of losses.

My grandfather would have assumed the correct record to be the 'official' one. Who could blame him? John's headstone may contain the wrong date.

It is of inordinate importance to me. Wrong, inaccurate, incorrect, no one's fault, doesn't really matter – except – John died 50 years ago this year. When? He may have lived ten days longer than we thought he did. I do realise my uncle would not have been celebrating Christmas 1943, but I have a personal fear of dying during the prelude to any Christmas. Afterwards is somehow better. Did he? Why did he have to die at all?

To have John back; to reverse history – to undo his final destiny, the hurt, the loss – is impossible. Bearing grudges of any kind does not facilitate these things, or achieve any useful purpose. There are, however, attempted justifications put forward sometimes by the Japanese, but more often than not by fellow Westerners, which stick in my gullet.

16

It is said that because of the Japanese culture – they are a medieval race with a different perspective, apparently – they do not have the same values or beliefs as us. Tosh. Their motivation as human beings during World War Two was exactly the same as anybody else's. Did they not demonstrate greed, self-gratification, humour (occasionally)? Did they not eat, sleep, bleed and visit the latrines? Were they not afraid, vulnerable to injury or disease and subservient to their masters? They worked to targets like some obscene parody of a modern day commercial sales office, didn't they?

Worst of all is the lame excuse that they considered 'surrender' to be dishonourable. Where is the documentation on mass suicides when Japan was defeated? Does this deep-rooted regulation only exist in their culture when they are the captors? I was taught that such a one way doctrine is called hypocrisy.

The term 'honourable' applied to the captives not the captors.

They did not emulate the bravery of their prisoners. They demonstrated weakness and showed exasperation at the strength and iron resolve of their 'slaves'. They did not display compassion or consideration.

I stress that reasons for the behaviour of the Japanese towards my uncle and his fellows have been unacceptably presented to me by my English peers. The Japanese don't mention it at all. There are no acceptable reasons, justifications, excuses or explanations, and 'sorry' seems so dreadfully inadequate.

Chapter 6

On the 27th of November 1993 I still haven't heard from the British Ambassador to Rangoon. I haven't found anyone who knew John. Sam Watson warned me that trails would run dry, and that I would become despondent, and that as soon as I thought I would never reach my goal, some fresh lead would suddenly materialise.

I've never weakened, nor lost sight of my quest at any time, but piecing together incidents from 50 years ago is a difficult job, and I understood that from the outset. To be honest, my progress seemed to be so successful at an earlier stage that I was astonished with my luck.

Spurred on again by Charles and by my dear husband, I'm pushing the boat out. Before receiving any further confirmation of John's whereabouts at given times, calls for men who remember him are going on to the 'grapevine'. According to Ann Apthorp, on Bob Grafton's death, the mantle of 'unofficial co-ordinator' of surviving British Sumatra Battalion members was taken up by Bill Little. Remarkably, another local man. I have written asking for his assistance in tracking down John's comrades.

The 'FEPOW Fulcrum', 'Legion' and 'Barbed Wire and Bamboo'(the organ of the Ex-POW Association of Australia) have all been called into service, now that I feel I have informative 'feelers' to put out. It's odd and extremely comforting that although I never sense John's disapproval or any impatience during lean spells of activity on his behalf, I always have this warm feeling of approval and encouragement when I leap into action. I wonder – just who is helping whom, here.

I'm back on the trail. I can look forward to illumination before too much longer. I will find out what happened to John and I will get to his grave. I can't reverse time and bring him back, but I can dot the 'i's' and cross the 't's' and neaten up history. What I would really like is to be serving John his Christmas dinner in four weeks time, but I can never have that.

One thing I did receive on the 10th of December was a letter from a gentleman in a remarkably similar situation to myself. Hugh Davies from Edmonton in Canada, whose uncle, Dawson Corbett of the Argyll & Sutherland Highlanders, lost his life at 26 at the Burma end of the line, and is buried in Plot B1, Row M, Grave 3 in Thanbyuzayat War Cemetery.

Firstly, to find another relative of a second wasted life has given me greater strength. There's safety in numbers and I was beginning to wonder where the first, second and third generations of the other 3,770 men had got to. I knew for certain that other lights would be burning, but to find one across the world was a sensation. Hugh doesn't know a lot about Dawson's time as a POW, and has actually asked for my help. I'm honoured. But he has achieved a remarkable feat. He's been to Thanbyuzayat and he's paid his tribute to his uncle.

"You can win the fight, you can grab a piece of the sky. You can break the rules but before you try – you've got to love someone." Elton John 1990

Hugh Davies' remarkable story began in exactly the same way as mine. His love and respect for a lost member of his family drove him to pursue a difficult trail and to enter 'forbidden' territory. He describes his 'illicit' travel experience as exciting and fun.

He also wrote of his adventure for publication in The Edmonton Journal, on the 31st of October 1993, and the opening paragraph of his story rings such familiar chords with me.

"It was easy enough to die building the Burma-Siam Railway under the Japanese in 1942–45. More than 16,000 British, Australian and Dutch POWs and between 80,000 and 100,000 Burmese and Malay labourers did so constructing a strategic link to India through mountainous, dense jungle in one of the worst climates in the world. However, visiting Thanbyuzayat War Cemetery at the northern end of the line in Burma – where my uncle is buried – is considerably more difficult".

Hugh, you took the words right out of my mouth, and you go on to say:
"Enquiries at Burmese Embassies are politely brushed aside on the grounds that Thanbyuzayat is 'off-limits' to foreigners because of 'insurgency problems'. In fact the majority of Burma is 'off-limits', and 'insurgents' and the 40 year unwillingness of the Burmese government to come to peaceful terms with them provide a convenient excuse for the continued hold on power by the Tatmadaw (Burmese Army) and its political arm, the State Law and Order Restoration Council (SLORC)."

Hugh, console yourself with the fact that your request to visit your uncle was politely brushed aside. Mine was completely ignored. But you finally made your visit and your Burmese travel agents had to acquire no less than eight government letters of permission addressed to the Township Police Stations, local SLORC offices, and commanders of the Army Regiments posted along the route south-east of Rangoon to Moulmein and Thanbyuzayat itself 40 miles further south.

Hugh set off with a driver and guide in June 1993 and they picked up their first armed escort on the Mon state border at the Sittang Bridge – the site of a bloody battle with the Japanese in February 1942. At Moulmein they were thoroughly quizzed by the ubiquitous Military Intelligence – young men recognisable despite plain clothes by dark glasses, mopeds and plastic 'leather' shoulder purses.

After an overnight stop, they set out in the morning for the cemetery, armed only with bunches of roses supplied by Burmese friends (an extremely hospitable race) and duly arrived at Thanbyuzayat. After 'checking in' at the local Tatmadaw garrison, permission to walk through the town was forbidden on the grounds that a bomb had been detonated there two months earlier. They provided a Toyota van-full of soldiers to escort Hugh to the cemetery.

As I have already said, Thanbyuzayat War Cemetery is beautiful and devotedly maintained, and this has been reaffirmed. Even in Hugh's presence, work was being done by local Burmese and he was, they said, only their second visitor in recent years, apart from diplomats making protocol calls.

John, hold tight, I'm not far away now. I'll be there soon. I'll bring you flowers and I'll bring you tributes and I'll bring you messages, but best of all, I'll bring you the undying love of your family.

I've found the tour company that can achieve the impossible very indirectly through the Foreign Office. The former suggested I contact Hugh Davies for research purposes and for a testimonial. He confirms them to be honest, efficient, courteous and totally reliable, and recommends them highly.

I have already been immunised against the obvious diseases such as polio, tetanus, typhoid and hepatitis. TB is worth being tested for as I am potentially at risk, I believe. All I really have to concern myself with is malaria and dysentery, especially as these killed John. They are still prevalent, of course.

Please God, don't let my mother find out about all these unlikely dangers until I'm safely home!

The only thing that really worries me is that after Hugh had finished his visit with his uncle, the Toyota van-full of soldiers invited him to buy them all lunch...

It is the 13th of December, and as the 27th approaches, the 50th anniversary of John's death, I am understandably taking stock of my feelings and of my progress, because what I do, I do for him – because he can't, and because I love him.

It is impatient of me to become frustrated with my research. I must remember that I'm dealing with history and with people whose vital recalled memories must take second place to the pressing demands of life, especially at this time of the year.

Eventually all will be revealed to me, I have no doubt at all, and it is a privilege for me to transmit and receive the details which will complete John's story. One critical source is John's brother, whom I know so very well since he is my dear papa. I am currently wrestling with the dire need to involve him in this great task, and a deep seated fear of bringing him distress. I'm working on it.

Honesty is of paramount importance with the nature of my undertaking and I feel that it is necessary to express the lows in addition to the highs and the breakthroughs.

Everything in existence has a parallel or an opposite, and I've been feeling those curious mixtures throughout. My preoccupation with whether or not I have received any post in the mornings generates equal emotions of pleasure and despondency. Lack of new evidence in correspondence is more than made up for by new leads or simply pleasure of contact. Out of the Burma-Siam Railway came death and deprivation overruled by strength, honour, understanding and triumph. Positive and negative. I bear no grudges that I inherited a negative bequest, and have received great joy from seeing it turned into positive benefit.

I regret, so badly, however, that I have my uncle's memory and not my uncle, and I would be lying if I said that his loss will not weigh heavily upon me this Christmas.

> *My dearest Uncle John,*
> *I looked at some wireless magazines today, knowing how much you liked to receive them when you were in Singapore. If you saw the price of them now you'd have a blue fit, but I'll buy the lot and send them out if you want them.*
>
> *My mum and dad are fine and they moved from your birth town this summer after 50 years in the house where I was born. It wasn't what it used to be, but only really changed recently, I'm happy to tell you. Your road stayed much the same for very many years.*

You'll be pleased, I know, that your other niece's second son was named after you and your brother, and takes after you in many ways. He looks a lot like you, too.

We all think about you a great deal and have your photos displayed because we're proud of you.

You know about my company and it's still doing well despite the recession. I was very pleased with the inspiration however, about the changes, which I made to excellent effect. Perhaps this was your accountancy training coming into its' own – thank you!

John, ever since I was a tiny little girl I've missed you. Please come home soon.

With all my love to you,

Mary

Even just before Christmas, in the last few days of post, some correspondence relating to John arrived on my door mat.

There was a delightful letter from Bill Little, (the Sumatra Battalion 'co-ordinator'), who didn't know John but assured me of the member's care for one another, because even within the group of 480 men there were of course individual groups who formed special friendships. It is just such other men who remember John I am hoping to track down.

An unprompted letter arrived from the Royal British Legion Pilgrimages Department on Christmas Eve. It wasn't personalised and it referred to a photograph enclosed of a grave 'in which I had expressed an interest'. Two things struck me about this letter. One was that it must have been sent to a significant number of other people since it was duplicated, and two, wondrous though it would have been to have received a photograph of John's grave three days before the 50th anniversary of his death, there was no photograph enclosed.

I also received some forms from the RAF Records Department to authorise the release of John's service record which I had requested. I was pleased to see that as his niece I was perfectly entitled to have these details, if they can find them, but my father, as John's brother, is naturally one step up in the pecking order of next of kin; no other relevant relatives remaining. I had to talk to my dad.

So I did, and wished I'd approached him before. We talked at length about my uncle, and I explained to him about the Sumatra Battalion, and told my father that the 27th was the day of the 50th anniversary of John's death. He signed the forms over our Christmas lunch table and it meant so very much to me to have his support, and to know that John had the power of his brother's love, directed at such an important time. My husband eventually relaxed, having looked very nervous about the possibility that I would push my luck to unreasonable limits.

My father can help me to finish John's story, and even if I cannot find a living soul who remembers him from the Burma end of the line, John will forgive me. His story will be complete. His brother knew him better than anyone else alive.

Two days later and suddenly it's the 27th of December; the day which I have quietly dreaded is one of those beautiful winter days which casts a misty sun through the trees and makes you feel good to be alive. Be at peace and live forever in our hearts, John.

Chapter 9

"We're feeding an economy that's got blood on it's hands." Midnight Oil. Sydney 1989

It is almost the New Year. I find the first stroke of Big Ben at midnight on New Year's Eve an emotionally charged moment – always. I have a secret dread of what might lie in wait, for all of us. But it is undoubtedly a time of new beginnings and a fresh start, and overall it is a pleasant occasion, worthy of great celebration.

1994 will certainly be a significant year for me. November, though it seems a long way off, will bring my pilgrimage to Burma to fruition. The monsoons will have ended, the cemetery restored to its former glory, and although I would have liked to have gone sooner, John has waited an awfully long time already. I don't think he will mind. The run-in is important for preparation, but could be brought forward or delayed depending on the whim of the Burmese Military at the time.

The situation in Lower Burma ranges from 'off limits' to 'not so off limits', and can change at a moments' notice. Permission to go must be grabbed with both hands.

Right Now Tours (Burma) is the unlikely sounding name of the company which will deliver me safely to fulfil my quest, and behind the company lies the most lovable maniac – Nicholas Greenwood. This accomplished travel writer has been conducting a passionate love affair with Burma, which he insists is purely platonic, for a number of years.

A delightful combination of Jewish Buddhist, Nicholas is able to achieve the 'impossible' because he has connections in Rangoon, from where all the necessary passes are obtained to facilitate travel to Moulmein and beyond. He can also help to obtain visas. Because the Burmese Military craves foreign currency via tourism but stringently avoid the indoctrination of their suppressed subjects by outside influences, they are in a cleft stick. A country with such an abysmal human rights record can hardly throw its doors open to the rest of the world, but would clearly like to.

The solution is an absurd compromise. They make it almost impossible to obtain permission to go, and then having relented they have you followed everywhere by secret police. According to Nicholas, the latter is not renowned for its discretion, and the temptation to wave to your obvious constant companions at your permanent rear is overwhelming.

Burma is, however, assuredly beautiful, fascinating, unspoiled and safe. I have nothing to fear. If, however, the Burmese or British authorities were aware of my plans I would be actively discouraged from making the trip. It is an understandable, yet preposterous state of affairs.

Worse, although I don't personally know other relatives of our lost men who wish to make a pilgrimage of their own, I'm absolutely convinced of their existence. What really troubles me is that among them there must still be many widows, who, despite suffering acute distress at having been unable to make the journey, in all fairness may not be up to its undertaking. And how can the British Government subsidise visits to a country ruled by bloodthirsty bandits?

I can't tell anyone about the mission until it is safely completed. A stampede for visas could put paid to any of them being issued and mass attention will send the Burmese right back into their shells and suddenly everything will be 'off limits' on a permanent basis. Little and often is the key, and I will share the means that I have found to go with all and sundry when the time is right. Unbelievably, 1995 has now been declared Myanmar (Burma) Tourism Year, although I'm not sure by whom, and perhaps this will serve to ease the flow of would-be visitors.

My reply from the British Embassy in Rangoon finally arrived in the New Year. Full of apologies for the delay, the British Vice Consul gave me a negative response to my request to visit concurrently with the Embassy officials' remembrance service on the grounds that these are not held annually. The last was in 1992 at Thanbyuzayat and plans to return there have not been made.

She also recommended that I contact Hugh Davies in Canada (my existing 'pen pal') for his help and advice, since the Embassy is aware of his visit last year. Well, isn't it a small world? Yet another indirect testimonial for the tour company which I have already found and clearly the only means to go.

Also enclosed with the letter were two photographs of John's grave. Many things went racing through my mind in all directions as I looked at them. Firstly, although I was aware of the grave's general appearance from seeing photographs of other headstones there, John's is exquisitely beautiful. It bears his name – my name. Then it hit me hard that he is buried within this site and that no mistake has been made. He died and he is buried.

I looked quickly at the date of his death, which is wrong – 17th December 1943. I looked at the message my grandfather had requested be inscribed – RIP. A simple epitaph which says it all and is so typical of my grandfather, who was the most apparently uncomplicated person I have ever met.

In both photographs, clearly visible, are the shadows and little brown feet of the Burmese, who so lovingly fulfil their duties to our men placed in their care forever. It seems that when an interest is shown from afar in a particular grave it creates much local excitement. With so few visitors dropping in the Burmese could be forgiven for thinking they are the custodians of forgotten remains.

There are shrubs visible on either side of John's headstone, as there are at all the grave sides, but the one to his left, which looks for all the world like a rose, contains one huge, cerise bloom which is leaning towards John's plaque very markedly.

So much information from a photographic image. It brought me closer to my goal just to look in isolation upon the scene of which I shall be a part before too much longer.

It also persuaded me that something I thought I might like to do must be done. The bronze plaque recording John's safekeeping in Thanbyuzayat War Cemetery for the last 50 years looks brand new. It must not, of course, be changed in any way. But the granite surround is sufficient to house a codicil.

The inscription contains a cross, the emblem of the RAF, his service number and rank. Initials, surname, service, wrong date of death, age 27, RIP.

J E Davey was not a number, he was John. His correct date of death must be recorded, but so too should his birth. There is also something more to be said; more pertinent now than it could ever have been before, the codicil will read:

A LIFE WHICH TOUCHES THE HEARTS OF OTHERS LIVES ON FOREVER

JOHN EDWIN DAVEY

28.10.16 – 27.12.43

I will take it with me and, heartily sick of bureaucracy, red tape and negative responses to requests born of love and caring, I shall 'super-glue' it to John's headstone when no one is looking.

With a long time to wait before this opportunity, and with absolutely no news and all sources apparently dry, I slapped another message on to Servicepals.

DOES ANYONE REMEMBER JOHN EDWIN DAVEY ("DAVE") FROM RAF SELETAR, THE BRITISH SUMATRA BATTALION ON THE BURMA-SIAM RAILWAY OR AT KHONKHAN? JOHN'S NIECE WANTS TO TELL HIS STORY – HE CAN'T. PLEASE HELP.

That ought to do it. Whilst waiting in the long Servicepals queue because of the D-Day anniversary this year, during which time they increased their pages considerably to cope with the demand, and more people would be tuning in than perhaps ever before, I prayed for a lucky break and then I went to Singapore.

Footsteps

It is the 26th of March 1994, and here I am en route to the Far East looking for – something. My father seems to understand my need to follow in his brother's footsteps, and I'm so glad of that.

Singapore has a lot to offer besides enabling me to trace the beginnings of John's end. The sun and rest won't go amiss, but I'm looking forward to seeing important landmarks and what I want to seek out is anything that remains as it was in the 1940s.

I'm sure I share something of John's spirit of adventure and intrigue at travelling across the world, although John would of course have gone by ship, and he would undoubtedly have been enthusiastic about his posting.

When the armed forces arrived to defend the island prior to capitulation, it must have caused them great consternation to see the RAF being evacuated on the same vessels which delivered them to their fate. Why men were left behind I have no idea, but as John was involved with the radar operation presumably this had to be wound down. Air reinforcements were promised but never came and the island fell to Japanese invading largely by bicycle. They must have been at least as astonished as the inhabitants of the 'impregnable fortress'.

Bridges

What a wonderful place Singapore is. Beautiful, friendly, cosmopolitan – cloudy – but that's got more to do with bad luck than the climate. You could describe the island uncharitably as a shopping centre with palm trees, because the jungle has gone and with it the swamps and the mosquitoes; high rise flats abound, but there is a special feeling about the place, and a very English one at that. No wonder John was happy here.

The humidity is pleasant, although the temperature changes quite quickly from bearable to sticky. John must have regularly lost several pounds in weight playing badminton here, which I'm sure he put back on in the canteen just as fast. I love the palm trees and the flowering shrubs.

We briefly toured the islands by junk which we boarded at Clifford Pier. Knowing that virtually everyone's escape from this island in 1942 was by any vessel to hand from this same pier gave me a knot in my stomach. I watched it fascinated as we pulled away and it disappeared into the distance.

Since so very little of the island would be recognisable to John, this one small structure is a link with the past. It is one of the bridges across time and space which I suppose I came here to find. Intrigued with this place we went back a second time and just sat watching the non-stop activity. I swear that a permanent impression of all the men who departed here lingers on. The atmosphere was tangible.

There were very many Japanese holidaying on the island which surprised me greatly. I found them unnerving, and it completely cramped smiling at your fellow holiday-makers across the crowded breakfast room. It made the whole affair seem even more utterly pointless and futile than it did already. I wished I had Superman's powers of time reversal. He was forbidden to use them but he still did so anyway to save Lois Lane.

Changi

The atmosphere at Changi is complicated by the fact that it is a working prison, containing Singapore's only gallows for the despatch of convicted drug traffickers. It is also, of course, closely guarded and out of bounds to visitors.

It stands hideously and largely obscured behind walling and is markedly the only structure which this country is prepared to let blacken with age. I can imagine the thinking behind this apparent neglect; that it makes the place appear even less desirable to the local population than even its purpose would surely do.

However, it is at odds with the shrine to the Allied POWs, frequently visited by loved ones and sympathisers alike, although there was no mistaking the heavy vibrations of this place, which are of both great peace and deep and irreparable sadness.

The history of Changi is fascinating, though. This north easterly part of the island once consisted exclusively of mangrove swamps and virgin forest, with trees over 100 feet high. The name 'Changi' comes from one of the tall timber trees which formerly abounded on the island.

In 1927 the site was selected for development as a military base. The strategic importance of Singapore had long been recognised although apparently it was never thought necessary to build fixed defences for the whole island. British eyes, however, viewed the Japanese with suspicion even at this time, and so coastal defences were to be established to protect the approach to the Jahore Strait and Changi's part was to house the Royal Artillery batteries covering the eastern approaches.

It was assumed then that any attack upon Singapore would come only from the sea, and this misapprehension unhappily seems to have stuck. This would be a reasonable assumption in view of Singapore being an island, were it not for the causeway which bonds it with the land mass of Malaysia.

By 1941, Changi Fortress, as the Japanese ironically termed it, was a thriving military base with enviable sports facilities and beautiful grounds. It offered a wonderful life style to servicemen and their families as did the rest of the island. All we saw was the jail and the chapel and the inevitable pink blocks of high rise flats with their washing poles standing to attention.

There was both a book to write in at the 'museum' and a hanging cluster of commemorative cards and it was satisfying to add John's name and my messages to him to both. I met a man who had lost his uncle, too.

Singapore is chock full of ghosts. Ghosts of the living as well as of the dead.

I felt closer to John than I've ever felt and my husband felt it, too. It was as if he was still there. If we could feel his presence so strongly in this place, then whatever would it be like in Burma?

I became finally convinced that the pilgrimage is necessary and the right thing to do. I got home safely from Singapore. John never did. Perhaps I brought something of him home from there and can do the same from Thanbyuzayat.

There *is* now a hotel at Moulmein, 40 miles north of Thanbyuzayat; complete with air conditioning, whilst the power is on. We were also offered an air conditioned car in which to make the pilgrimage, but it seems more appropriate to sweat it out on the train – if it runs. Burma does not have timetables. We've been allotted our guide, the itinerary is prepared, but you cannot *book* until a few weeks before you are scheduled to go. November the 17th is the day of the trip. On Tuesday the 22nd of November I finally get to John.

Myanmar Tourism Year has been postponed until 1996. Someone has realised just in time that declaring it, and fulfilling the resultant obligations, are two different things.

Chapter 11

Four weeks after returning from Singapore, my Servicepals message went out at last. I had been tuning in, but Charles Peall still spotted it before I did and telephoned me to let me know. The week went by and nothing happened. I thought the worst.

On Bank Holiday Monday, the 2nd of May, I received a phone call. It was from Mrs Arthur Hargest, whose husband was a Corporal in the RAF and knew John both at RAF Seletar and in Burma. He too was a member of the British Sumatra Battalion and he is now 83 years old. I have found him at last. I've struck gold, because if he is able to help me, he will have the answers to almost all my questions about John's last years.

Why were John and his unit left behind by the RAF? How did he escape to Sumatra? Did he keep his sense of humour? Did he drive his comrades nuts beating *them* at sports? Did he really die of dysentery? Did he die alone? What was he like? Was he as wonderful as *I* think he is?

I have written to Mr Hargest and I hope that when he knows a little more about me he might agree to meet me. I cannot believe my luck and it proves that you must never, ever give up on anything, no matter what the odds against success.

I have never had the opportunity to know John and to enjoy his company, but at least I know two men who between them understood him very well. My father's memories of John span his earliest years, when little brothers are a species all of their own. My dad saw him mature without fully noticing that he had and his recall is naturally of John's early development when his charactcristics wcrc forming. In their twenties they didn't see a great deal of one another and once the war began they spent long periods apart.

Arthur Hargest saw John blossom in a posting which suited him well. He was working with radios and in his element and he was being paid as well. John took full advantage of the sports facilities and had pride in his fitness and the whole social scene of the services would have developed friendships and camaraderie which they would have shared. Only Arthur can tell me how John reacted to capture and to a drastically reduced diet and to slave labour and to tropical disease. A very different person would have emerged to the one my father knew, with all his strengths stretched to their limits.

I will hear from him soon, and with his kind co-operation I can achieve just what I set out to do. I can reconstruct my uncle's persona, and know what I have missed.

Only now can I admit, even to myself, that the odds against finding Arthur were incalculable.

———————

During my first telephone conversation with Mr Hargest's wife, I cried. When my husband saw my face afterwards he knew exactly the nature of the call I had received – which was fortunate. I couldn't speak.

Arthur must have been astonished at my Servicepals message. He doesn't always look at it and has only really started to do so recently. To see simultaneous references to the RAF, of which he was a member; Seletar, his base in Singapore; the Burma-Siam Railway, of which he was a victim; the British Sumatra Battalion, who gave him some semblance of order, and John Edwin Davey, a lost comrade, must have seemed extraordinary to him.

To say that his response was extraordinary for me is an understatement. The 480 men of the Battalion were whittled down to 327 through death in captivity alone. Heaven knows how many more have departed in the last 50 years. Only a few men may have known my uncle personally and one of them, I knew, had died in 1966.

I had become reluctantly resigned to accepting defeat and making the best job I could of an unfinished story, when Arthur came along at last. I was incredibly excited at the prospect of meeting him.

When I did, I was so glad that John had had such a man as a close friend. I liked him very much and appreciated in particular the fact that he was open and honest with me. He began by saying that he didn't think he could help me very much and then proceeded to unveil significant amounts of valuable information. He answered every single question I had prepared for him and filled in a great deal of detail besides.

Anecdotes came forward which were just the sort of memories I was hoping for. Recollections which gave substance to my uncle's character, provided positive proof that John was every bit as special as I thought he was. And all the time, I realised how lucky John was to have Arthur around.

I am also able, at last, to begin John's story, since I now have some crucial missing components, despite still having more questions. Arthur told me that since they had worked with John as fellow radio operators on a daily basis, I should try to find Joe White and Harry Strike. My heart leapt and sank simultaneously. Where on earth was I to find them?

Amongst the three photographs of John with mates in Singapore which I took with me to show to Arthur, there was one of him with John. Neither of us were all that surprised.

———————

What did surprise me was receiving a letter from Sgt R S Anderson of the 80 Anti-Tank Regiment, who did not know John, but was writing to offer his kind assistance in response to my request for information, published in the 'FEPOW Fulcrum', seven months after its submission.

I can personally vouch for this wonderful publication and the worthwhile wait for inclusion in view of great demand. Now I know why. In the next post I received a letter from Bob Bush who not only knew John at 250 AMES (Air Ministry Experimental Station) but was with him when he died. Of all the ex-FEPOWs I had dreamt of embracing and having the honour to know, the mate who was with John when it really mattered, if he'd been with one at all, was the ultimate prize.

As if this were not a miracle enough in itself, Bob included in his letter the address of one of John's work mates, whom Arthur had mentioned, Joe White. This went far beyond coincidence and good fortune. This was God given.

I telephoned Bob that morning. We spoke for a good hour. What Bob told me was incredible. The gaps were filling fast. John's story, as he would wish me to tell it, was blossoming faster than I could write it down. But as Bob made clear, despite his fond memories of John, which were of a gentle, immensely popular man, Joe knew him even better. So too did Jim Hall, another radio operator with whom John worked as mechanic.

Bob had already arranged to meet Joe on the 2nd of August. I unashamedly gate-crashed, and then cheekily called for Jim's presence, too. Bob was thrilled. The man they knew as 'Dave' could not be a part of their reunions, but his niece could. They accepted me willingly and unreservedly. I was overjoyed.

The next day, the 29th of June, I saw my father. Nothing on earth would have prevented me from telling him that I'd found no less than *three* of John's other mates, including the man who was with John at the end. When I told him about my meeting with them my father asked me if he could join us. I don't think I need to explain the significance of this, my pleasure at the prospect, or how much we all looked forward to the 2nd of August.

In the meantime, Arthur's recollections, Sgt Anderson's assistance and Peter Dunstan's brilliant maps of Sumatra had pieced together the escape route of the men posted to Singapore before the capitulation. Peter has a copy of "Singapore's Dunkirk", now sadly out of print, which confirms it.

I then received yet another letter, from J A McCall, a Navy member of the Battalion from Northern Ireland. The kindness of these men knows no bounds and I fully appreciate the honour of corresponding with the men who appear in Dudley Apthorp's Nominal Roll, alongside John.

And then the final letter dropped onto my threadbare doormat. From Raymond Frazer, recalled most fondly by Bob Bush and Arthur Hargest and doubtless many more, who was honoured after the war for his efforts in the evacuation from Singapore to save others. His own input on John was equally remarkable, and, apart from a few minor queries, which I now felt could be cleared up very easily by comparing evidence, and in a few incidences simply putting two and two together, I had the lot.

This was a most weird time for me. Everything seemed to be coming together in a great rush, and I had to battle for time and space in which to evaluate it all and to make the very best of this wonderful opportunity.

Firstly, I was simply overwhelmed at the willingness of these great men who had suffered so badly, to give freely of their time and experiences to share with someone they did not know. I knew that they were exceptional human beings, but their compassion and warmth still took me totally by surprise. I should have known that there could be such an affinity with Battalion members, since both Charles Peall and Peter Dunstan have become my own mates and yet they were at the Thailand end of the line.

Then I appreciated fully that although conditions differed, and circumstances to a degree, this whole line which crossed two countries was one and the same. The locations and sometimes treatment varied, but the nightmare was the same.

If I had been reconstructing John's story like a jig-saw puzzle, I could never be sure that I would find all of the pieces. Yet they appeared to be complete as they became firmly placed in position.

I had met the man who last saw John as his illness struck, before it had won, and John had lost. I had found two men who had been with him at the end. I knew what had killed my uncle and how he had died.

A sort of divine acceptance, a quiet and woeful rigidity gripped me then. I saw the light; really saw for the first time what John's story – the Burma-Siam Railway – was all about. Through a deep, personal understanding of the fate which befell him, I had at last achieved total empathy with his soul. All was calm then, as if we had truly met each other on middle ground.

When I began my long search for knowledge, I had not realised fully that John and his comrades, known and unknown, and on both ends of the line, had conducted their nightmare in one of the most beautiful places in the world. Hell against a background of supreme beauty. This was the ultimate technicolour nightmare. Different to the black and white images which portray the mud-filled trenches of World War One, but every bit as terrible.

If John had decided to give up and die, in the circumstances in which he found himself, no one on earth would have blamed him. No intelligent human being would accuse him of weakness. But he didn't want to die. He meant to get out of that 'death house' alive. He meant to get back to his mates and to go home. John wanted to live. It was too late for him. Too little, too late.

There was a time, not so very long ago, when I could not understand why some men made it back and some did not. How some men extricated themselves from the very jaws of death and John could not. It was during this most memorable phase of my research, which has marked the course of my life forever, that I finally understood the reality of it all. Given such appalling circumstances in which to become seriously ill, a toss of the coin would decide whether you lived or whether you died, because the whole ghastly bad dream was conducted upon the very knife edge of existence.

Instead of asking myself repeatedly why John had not made it home; rather than reckoning with some unseen menace as to why my precious uncle had not lived, it was so much more appropriate to ask how the hell anybody had made it out of there alive.

The fact that my beloved uncle fought so hard to keep his life intact and return to normality adds much fuel to the inferno of guilt of his captors. The Japanese may as well have put a gun to John's head and pulled the trigger, and it would have been no more cruel and destructive had they done so.

If the withholding of adequate supplies of nutritious food was inhumane (and in the case of Red Cross parcels this was denial of the worst order), then the refusal of drugs and medicines with which to treat the sick was criminal negligence. Men became sick because of lack of food and overwork in the first place, rendering them weak and their natural defences unable to protect them from the onslaught of even worse disease. To compound this by giving even less nutrients and denying any effective treatment was pre-determined murder.

Contrition to create the most extraordinary set of circumstances in which to play Russian roulette with the lives of the most innocent and noble victims was their crime.

Part II **John's Story**

"He was mature, even tempered, good humoured and good company." Arthur Hargest

"Your uncle was a very popular member of 250 AMES. He was quietly spoken and had a lovely nature." Bob Bush

"He was a delightful, quiet man. Very well liked. I will always remember your uncle. He was a softly spoken young man who never hurt a soul." Raymond Frazer

"In everything he said and everything he did, he was a gentleman." Joe White

"And you can tell everybody, this is your song ...... I hope you don't mind if I put down in words how wonderful life is when you're in the world." Elton John 1969

"What was John like?" I asked my father. "A little sod", he replied.

In 1916 Rasputin was murdered by Russian nobles. The House of Commons voted overwhelmingly for military conscription, deeming that voluntary effort was not enough to win the war and that there must be compulsion on those shirking their duty. 'British summer time' commenced with the introduction of clocks being put forward one hour in an effort to save hundreds of thousands of tons of coal. The Somme campaign opened and Lloyd George became Prime Minister.

Over 50,000 cases of syphilis were reported among British servicemen, and the Coca-Cola Company introduced a new contoured bottle to make imitation difficult. (Nothing new under the sun).

The price of a loaf of bread reached record levels at ten pence – a serious blow when the poorest in the nation could not afford anything else. The procedure by which internal organs could be photographed – the X-ray – was discovered. "If you were the only girl in the world" and "Take me back to dear old Blighty" were 'top of the pops'.

The British casualties in August alone in World War One totalled 127,000, and the years' other deaths included Henry James, Field Marshal Earl Horatio Herbert Kitchener, Austro-Hungarian Emperor Franz Josef, British pharmaceuticals manufacturer Sir Joseph Beecham and Jehovah's Witnesses founder, Charles Taze Russell.

The year heralded the births of Francois Mitterrand, Harold Wilson, Robert MacNamara, Sir Yehudi Menuhin, and on the 28th of October 1916, John Edwin Davey was born, with mid-brown hair and hazel eyes.

John was the youngest son, by 15 months, of Charles Frank and Edith Emilie Davey, and brother to William Francis Davey. His father was English and his mother half-French and half-Irish. My grandmother's maiden name was Crozier.

John had two aunties. Molly, on his mother's side, and Nellie on his father's, and a gorgeous little boy he was, with a face like an angel, and the disposition of, well – a little brother. Both John and his brother William were boys to be proud of, and their mother adored them. Like many loving mums, especially of her era, she made the best of whatever came her way to feed and clothe her war babies, and she did a grand job.

During the first year of John's life, *John Fitzgerald Kennedy, Shrimata Indira Gandhi, Robert Mitchum and Dizzy Gillespie were born. Rodin, Scott Joplin, US Colonel William F Cody, alias Buffalo Bill, German Count Ferdinand von Zeppelin and Mata Hari, died.*

Lloyd George appealed to the nation to subscribe to War Loans, issued to finance the war, the cost of which was running at a staggering £5.7 million per day. The men and women of the country were called upon to shorten the war and save the lives of the brave young men at the front by investing five shillings, for which they would receive 5.25% interest per annum over 30 years.

John's father was a carpenter. Sometimes he had work and sometimes he didn't. In 1918 the government launched its two-meatless-days a week policy, designed to deal with a grave food shortage. This somewhat presupposed that you could afford meat for the remaining five. My father contracted rickets.

The Red Baron died as did Claude Debussy. The school leaving age was increased to 14. All was not well on the Western front, where the Germans took 80,000 Allied prisoners in France. This year also saw the birth of the Royal Air Force from a marriage between The Royal Flying Corps and the Royal Naval Air Service, brought about more out of a desire for revenge against the German raids on London than for any strategic or tactical reasons.

New Allied tactics had the Germans on the run before the end of the year and November heralded Armistice, victory and jubilation. The cost in human lives of the Great War? Ten million. Top of the pops? "After you've gone". Women voted for the first time in a general election. The Coalition Government led by Lloyd George triumphed.

John was teasing, badgering and generally irritating to his brother. As he evolved he developed a good sense of humour, but according to my father, he was still irritating. His general demeanour was 'nice' and he was not a moody person. Like all of us, there were times when John was quiet and reflective. My father must have looked forward to these rare respites.

Born in Croydon, John and my father lived in or around Croydon for most of their early lives. Very different to the Croydon of today, my grandfather's personal memories of the town in which I was born held my fascination whilst he graced our lives. Much of it had been arable land, beautiful old buildings and areas of great colour, where infamous characters such as 'clay pipe Alice' adorned the neighbourhood.

After the Great War, my forebears deserved the Great Peace, *but 1919 saw Lenin seeking to spark revolution in Europe, since Russia was still in the grip of civil war and the founding of the Fascist Party by Benito Mussolini. These were hard times to be born, but for 'your entertainment', Mary Pickford, Douglas Fairbanks, Charles Chaplin and D W Griffith formed United Artists.*

An Irish Terrier bit a small white dog in Surrey, Croydon's county, which led to a rabies scare, and the muzzling of 850,000 British dogs. Jack Dempsey won the world heavy weight championship, Renoir died and "I'm forever blowing bubbles" hit the charts.

The Roaring Twenties got off to a fine start with prohibition in the States. Fortunately, Croydon was exempt from this. Adolf Hitler made his debut in Germany with anti-Jewish propaganda and Albert Hill won two Olympic gold medals for Britain on the track. Mary Pickford married Douglas Fairbanks and the miners went on strike. The IRA killed fourteen soldiers and the quote of the year was attributed to H L Mencken in the U.S. "Puritanism: the haunting fear that someone, somewhere, may be happy".

1921 saw the introduction of the first birth control clinic in London, against the better judgement of both doctors and the clergy. Dr Marie Stopes realised her ambition to protect women such as my grandmother from the burden of child bearing when they could ill afford the babes already in their care, with the cervical cap and other cheap contraceptive methods which were available at the time.

The year also saw skirts rise (revealing the calves of women's legs) and morals decline. Utah considered imprisoning inappropriately dressed women. In truth, it was the flat chested, straight clothed and short haired image, reflecting their new 'freedom' which was ruffling male feathers.

The Communist Party formed in China, Caruso died, and, surprise, surprise, a census revealed a drop in the birth rate and a population growth lower than in any previous ten year period. Day tripping boomed. The Davey's couldn't afford holidays but they knew how to have a good time all the same and John and my father enjoyed outdoor pursuits and the good old fashioned activity unknown to today's kids – reading books.

Crown Prince Hirohito was named Regent of Japan, at the age of 20. John was five years old.

Chapter 2

Two little boys

Money troubles dogged 1922 and the German mark went into free fall against the dollar and halved its value in ten days. The German's sought to defer their war debts which angered the French, who threatened to cease their own payments to Britain if Germany didn't pay up. Britain pointed out that it owed money to America so reparations payments would have to continue. So other than death and debt not a lot had been achieved.

Lloyd George resigned and Andrew Bonar Law was requested by the King to form a new Tory government.

George Cadbury died and the Reader's Digest was born. Sixteen steps were discovered in the Valley of the Kings which led Lord Carnarvon and Howard Carter to the final resting place of Tutankhamun.

On the 3rd of November, Patricia Mary Salter was born in Ivybridge in Devon; my mother.

The New Year brought mourning in Paris for Sarah Bernhardt's death, the marriage between Lady Elizabeth Bowes-Lyon and The Duke of York and the price of a loaf in Germany to 201,000,000,000 marks.

300,000 died in the earthquake in Tokyo. The further disasters of typhoons, flooding and epidemics sent one million refugees into the countryside. Those who remained joined two-mile-long queues for a daily riceball.

Stanley Baldwin was made Prime Minister on the diagnosis of Mr Law's terminal throat cancer and subsequent resignation. Hitler led his first Nazi Party rally in Munich and the Ku Klux Klan claimed one million members. "Who's sorry now" was a hit of 1923.

My grandfather cannot get work. The Davey's have had enough and decide to seek their fortunes in New Zealand. On the 3rd of March 1924, Charles Frank, Edith Emilie, William Francis and John Edwin leave England bound for Napier.

My poor grandmother was not a good sailor and suffered dreadfully from seasickness. No doubt seven year old John was up on deck learning the tricks of winning at deck tennis and quoits.

William Francis Davey, John's elder brother, takes up the story in his own words.

"John and I were born at Whitehorse Road, Croydon. Memories of our earliest years are somewhat vague but I recall that our father took a trip to New Zealand. We had friends living there who had emigrated previously.

40

Meantime John and I had commenced our education at a small church school in nearby
Selhurst. Dad returned after a year in New Zealand determined that we should emigrate.

In March 1924 the Davey family set sail aboard the 'SS Ruahini' bound for New Zealand via
the Panama Canal.

An ocean liner and a voyage half across the world seemed paradise indeed for small boys. My
brother and I soon befriended three slightly older boys, the only other children on board, and
fell under their baleful influence.

Our usual preoccupations included such delights as leaving the taps running to flood
bathrooms or joining hands and connecting ourselves to the ship's electricity supply –
fortunately for us a mere 110 volts – for a daily 'boost'. Other activities are best left
undescribed. I can only imagine the relief amongst the stewards and cabin staff at the end of
the voyage.

We disembarked at Wellington, the capital and a notoriously windy city. Thence we travelled by
train to Napier some 200 miles to the north.

Napier is situated on the coast at Hawkes Bay a few miles from Cape Kidnappers, associated
forever with Captain Cook. In 1924, with a population of only a few thousand, Napier was a
pleasant coastal town with an impressive pine fringed marine parade, some one and a quarter
miles in length.

The town had a typical colonial character, the majority of houses being detached single storey
buildings of timber construction, white painted and with either red or green painted
corrugated iron roofs. The local people were friendly and we soon felt at home.

John and I began to enjoy the open air life and even came to accept the paradox of Christmas
occurring at midsummer!

The years passed happily and we soon felt we were New Zealanders. With the sea on our
doorstep as it were and a river close by, we had quickly learned to swim and in the summer
our days were spent either in the water or cycling to local beauty spots.

New Zealand is a unique and beautiful country with rich and varied scenery ranging from
pasture-land, thickly wooded areas, thermal regions with geysers and boiling pools and
impressive mountain ranges. The tip of the North Island is virtually sub-tropical. The lower
regions of the South Island in contrast are much cooler, with glaciers and fjords on the coast.

In the 1920s Napier was well equipped with schools, there being three primary schools with mixed classes and boys' and girls' high schools. The high schools were quite large, the boys' school catering for up to 600 pupils including boarding facilities for some 300 pupils from outlying areas.

In 1929 at the age of 14 I started my first year of secondary education in Form 3a, John following me a year later. There was considerable emphasis on sporting activities with one being compulsory – rugby! A medical certificate was necessary to avoid participation. The fact that a country with a population in the 1930s of less than two million came to dominate world rugby is no doubt due in some measure to such a philosophy.

Swimming was another activity encouraged by the school. Our PT Instructor, an Australian ex-mounted policeman of Teutonic extraction, with, to say the least, a somewhat forbidding personality, remains forever in my memory.

The nearest mountain range, snow-capped during the winter, was just 50 miles away. In early spring, as soon as the last snows disappeared, our Australian friend would take us swimming in the local river which bordered the school grounds.

We were required to strip naked, towels and costumes forbidden, plunge into the icy cold stream and swim for ten minutes or so. The session would end with 30 or so boys – the large, the small, the burly and the skinny – running up and down the river bank until dry enough to don their clothes and return to class.

Life was good, life was earnest, life was fun!

In 1931 I was in form 5a. At morning parade on the playing fields in front of the school building on the first day of the second term, the earthquake struck. The epicentre was later calculated to have been a mile or so offshore and was the severest earthquake at that time recorded in the Southern Hemisphere. The initial shocks were so powerful that we were flung to the ground. The earth literally rippled and cracks appeared everywhere.

We were instructed to proceed home immediately and needed no second bidding. John and I left in some trepidation but were relieved to find our house intact and our mother somewhat frightened but safe.

The shopping centre, with the possible exception of any brick built buildings, would have no doubt survived, but fires started in one or two establishments resulting in complete destruction of the town centre. Mercifully, the death toll was very low.

"Two little boys".

John is to the right whilst my father advertises Persil to the left.

Charles Frank, Edith Emilie, William Francis, John Edwin.

My grandfather with my father on his bicycle.

John with his mother to the right and an unknown lady to the left.

John, "Billy" and an unknown admirer.

My grandfather with his young sons at a Napier beauty spot.

Target practise.

Severe tremors occurred for several days after the initial shock wave and with water and power supplies disrupted, it was decided that women and children should be evacuated. Thus John and I and our mother were despatched to Havelock North, a town south of Napier.

Hopes of a respite from the tedium of school work were quickly dispelled and my brother and I became temporary boarders at the local high school. After some three months we returned to resume our lives at Napier.

Our father was a carpenter and after the earthquake was quite busy as there was much rebuilding work. A temporary shopping centre was erected consisting of wooden buildings built around a square base and surrounded by a wooden boardwalk, reminiscent of a typical wild west town.

Life in Napier gradually settled down again but the family fortunes began to take a turn for the worse. Jobs became scarce and our mother became more and more homesick. Encouraged by letters from her sister, who lived in Bristol, she eventually persuaded dad to return to England. Thus in September 1932 we booked passage home aboard the 'SS Rangitata', again via the Panama Canal.

John and I, now 16 and 17 respectively, left New Zealand with mixed emotions. We were sad to leave our many school friends yet were young enough to view the forthcoming voyage as an exciting adventure.

I had said goodbye to my particular friend about a week before our departure. He was embarking on a motorcycle trip to Lake Taupo, New Zealand's largest lake and a popular tourist area situated almost exactly in the centre of the North Island.

John's closest friend lived a mile or so along the coast at a small farming settlement. My last memories of leaving Napier are of my brother's friend standing forlornly at the trackside to wave his farewells to John as we headed north by train to Auckland. There, after an overnight stay, we boarded the 'Rangitata'.

Again we were the youngest passengers aboard and filled our days with swimming in the open air pool on the top deck or playing deck quoits or deck tennis, becoming quite expert at both pursuits. John was a tricky customer, particularly at deck tennis and could usually beat me. Together, we were a match for the other passengers.

The sea journey from New Zealand to England normally took from four to five weeks depending on weather conditions. This may seem ridiculous when compared to modern air travel but the sea voyage offers the comfort of a hotel, good food and facilities for indoor and outdoor pursuits and, for the young at least, the prospect of adventure.

Furthermore, it gives one a sense of perspective. To stand on deck at night, as I did on more than one occasion, during an electrical storm with the horizon visible at each lightning flash certainly gave one pause to think how infinitely small is man.

On the Pacific crossing from New Zealand to Panama the only land you see is Pitcairn Island, one time temporary home to Fletcher Christian and his fellow mutineers from the 'Bounty'. Liners normally anchored off shore at Pitcairn. This enabled the native traders to come alongside in their canoes to sell their wares, chiefly fruit and trinkets, to the passengers.

After the brief diversion of Pitcairn came the long haul to Panama where we were granted the respite of eight hours on shore to discover the delights of Panama City. John and I with our parents enjoyed our day and duly returned to our ship. I staggered on board with a huge bunch of bananas, purchased cheaply at the dockside, but by the next morning they had turned black and had to be consigned to a watery grave.

The passage through the canal is spectacular if at times a trifle laborious. One soon appreciates the engineering skill that must have been required in its construction.

After leaving the canal we picked up speed and the journey across the Atlantic was under way. Storms delayed our crossing and we were several days late in reaching England.

John and I had by now only the vaguest memories of our life in England, and viewed our return 'home' with anticipation and some anxiety. We were met on arrival by our mother's sister, together with our uncle and our cousin Tom and travelled with them by train to Bristol.

Happy days in New Zealand.

With a little friend in New Zealand, my father does a very passable impression of James Dean with John to the left.

On board the 'Rangitata', homeward bound. John is on the left of the middle row. My father is back right with my grandfather behind him.

Tom had two sisters, both in their twenties, so their family of five was increased to nine by our arrival. However their house was of reasonable size and we were successfully accommodated. John and I shared Tom's bedroom, two folding bed-chairs being pressed into service.

Tom, who was still attending college in Bristol, was a lively outgoing character and we three became close friends.

I remember we would read to each other until the early hours. We would take turns on successive nights, one of us reading to the other two. "The Gorilla Hunters" by R M Ballantyne and "She" by Rider Haggard are titles I recall. I can still, after all these years, hear my uncle calling out to us to keep 'b....y' quiet on more than one occasion.

During our stay in Bristol Dad returned to Croydon to find accommodation for the family and after a pleasant three months in Bristol we settled down again in Croydon. We had left New Zealand partly because of the economic situation only to find on our return that things were also depressed in England, particularly in the building trade.

Our schooling had been interrupted at a somewhat critical stage by our hasty departure from New Zealand, but it became obvious that my brother and I would need to find employment to reinforce the family finances. I managed to find a job in the costing office of a large cabinet manufacturing firm in Croydon while John became articled to an accountant in London.

In 1935 we moved to a house in Thornton Heath, north of Croydon. My job in Croydon had finished, and to my delight a local firm who specialised in radio servicing offered me employment.

John and I were both interested in radio and it became our absorbing hobby. I built several radio receivers starting with simple battery powered types and then going on to more ambitious projects. In those days there were intriguing shops which sold radio components and materials and were a hobbyist's dream.

While I concentrated on radio receivers and amplifiers, John became a short wave freak. At night he would listen in on headphones scouring the airwaves for signals from overseas amateur transmitters. He would awaken me on occasion with calls such as 'Hey – I've got Kuala Lumpur' and I would retort with 'serves you right – now let me get some sleep'.

Meanwhile, cousin Tom and his family moved from Bristol and bought a house about a mile from our home. We three boys spent happy times together camping or going on cycle trips to the Surrey countryside at weekends. The next few years passed pleasantly, if uneventfully, until September 1939. England was at war with Germany.

48

Tom, who was an enthusiastic member of the Territorials at school joined the army, but was unhappily discharged as unfit after a few months due to complications from a previous leg injury sustained while motor cycling when he was 19 years old.

Meanwhile, John and I decided to join the RAF as, not surprisingly, radio mechanics. It was our intention to enlist together in the hope that as brothers we might be able to serve together.

Unfortunately, I succumbed to an attack of influenza with the result that I enlisted some two weeks later than John. He had taken a trade test and was accepted as a radio mechanic and, after initial training known colloquially as 'square bashing', was posted to the RAF radio school at Yatesbury near Calne in Wiltshire.

In the meantime, having proved that I could breathe and stand on one leg without falling over, I was passed A1 and enlisted as a wireless operator. After kitting out at Cardington and drilling for two weeks on the sea front at Morecambe, I spent the next three months at Debden in Essex. Debden was a fighter station with Hurricane Squadrons and while there I was attached to the station fire crew.

Before leaving Debden, from where I was to be posted to the wireless operators' training school at Compton Bassett, I applied for a 24 hour pass to visit my parents.

To my great delight I found on arrival that John was there. He had been on leave and had to report back to camp the next morning. As we had not seen each other since our enlistment, we talked into the small hours recounting our RAF experiences to date.

In the morning we said our farewells and wished each other luck. We pledged to 'see you when it's all over'.

I never saw John again."

John Edwin Davey displayed all outward signs of being fearless. Deep down inside, like everybody else, he was rather more complex and undoubtedly deep.

There was a tremendous self-sufficiency about my uncle, and my father is convinced that he would not have married. There were girls who had designs on John, whom he perceived as 'giggling tarts', but he certainly enjoyed a very healthy relationship with his mother, and empathy with her character, and he did not have a problem with women.

John also got along extremely well with his father. My grandpa was a very laid-back sort of person. I never once saw him lose his temper or appear in a bad mood or be anything other than his normal, placid self, in all the years I knew him. He lived to the extraordinary age of 97 and sort of fluttered out like a used up candle. There was nothing at all wrong with him, although some hardening of the arteries caused him to see sparrows on the end of his hospital bed, but only at the end. And no one could wish for a more peaceful end. He just went, with a smile on his face and a pretty nurse in attendance.

He spoke of John retrospectively with great affection and as if he were a friend. I don't suppose for a moment my grandfather did not feel very deep emotions, but he didn't show them, at least never to me, other than his love. It wasn't that he was a stiff-upper-lip Englishman – far from it; it was just that he didn't seem to have anything bad, cross or negative to say about anything.

He was a good father and he loved both his sons. Although John's mother had a particular affinity with her younger son, which my father recognised, she idolised my father. When it came to natural pairing off it would be Emilie and Billy, Charles and John who 'ganged' up together. Although John's looks came mostly from his mother's side, his character was probably more aligned with his father's.

My grandmother was very close to her sister, Molly. They came to England together without their parents, presumably from Ireland. My father isn't sure, and he never met his grandparents on his mother's side and no photographs remain of them. This is a pity, because I'm sure that Emilie's French father and Irish mother contributed a lot to the genetic melting-pot.

Emilie and Molly had jobs before their marriages, at the tea-rooms on Victoria Station where they once met Charlie Chaplin.

Even though money was tight, work was scarce and two world wars meant a general shortage of food and other provisions, my grandmother truly could make a silk purse out of a sow's ear. She was a wonderful cook and seamstress.

Molly had two daughters and a son; Babs, Pinkie and Tom; cousins to John and my father. Tom married Edna, who has told me she was very fond of my grandmother, who made the most wonderful teas which she can still remember. Tom is also now absent without leave from the family, as are his sisters, and his humour is something I will always remember and laugh about out loud when no one else knows why, when I suddenly recall the things he came out with. The combination of Tom and my father was positively lethal.

John engaged in pillow fights with his brother in their youth, and they would talk a lot after 'lights out' when they were supposed to be asleep. They didn't clash politically and generally got along extremely well. They shared a lot of common interests, specifically radios.

In the 30s, after their return from New Zealand, John applied to some extraordinarily long distance stations to report his reception of their programmes. He kept their replies for a short while, and so I'm able to record that he made contact with New York, Pennsylvania, Cuba, Sydney, Victoria and Columbia. And thanks to John filing the latter acknowledgement card back-to-front, I can see that it was addressed to Sr John E Davey, Norbruny (Norbury) Avenue, Yhonlon Hearz (Thornton Heath), Suney (Surrey). Testimony to the skills of the Post Office in 1935.

According to my father, John was 'crafty' at sports. There was no rivalry between them and John's brother conceded that he was very athletic. He had supremely mastered those shots in badminton that land just on the other side of your opponent's net, which caused me to give up the game some years ago. My brother is also a good player and it would have been most interesting to see them compete. I hate to say this but my money would have been on my uncle.

John had a very good appetite and he slept peacefully and quietly. He enjoyed reading books on animals and natural history. and novels by Joseph Conrad. Musically, I know that John especially liked 'The Haunted Ballroom' by Geoffrey Toye, a very English composer who coincidentally died in 1942. It is a beautiful piece of music, which I unknowingly acquired in 1973.

There was a very strong bond between John and my father, even though like most men John was not particularly demonstrative to his male relations and there were some differences in their characters.

John possessed a completely neutral accent, in common with the rest of my family. How we achieved this with our South London background is probably due to the combined influences of the West Country, France, Ireland and New Zealand and a long line of mysteriously neutrally speaking predecessors. What a cosmopolitan lot we are.

John didn't drink and he didn't smoke. It is unlikely that he availed himself of the cigarettes so generously donated by the Burmese priests on the Burma-Siam Railway. He wasn't one for going out a great deal, although like almost everyone of his era, John made an exception for the pictures. Films with Boris Karloff and American musicals, such as 42nd Street. He would only tease his closest friends. He would open up completely to people he knew and liked but not to strangers or people outside his circle.

John's teasing stopped with his maturity. It became an affectionate humour then, shared only with his special friends. He had a perfectly healthy irreverence towards authority, although my father felt that John could be prudish when it came to anything of which he intrinsically disapproved, such as my father's quite normal penchant for the fairer sex. It was particularly painful for my dad to learn, that John had sought confirmation, and the Holy Communion, whilst a prisoner of war.

As a boy, John had acquired a thick lip in response to his campaign of aggravation. He was extremely intelligent and creative, but at school he was inclined to look out of the window whilst 'Billy' got top marks, and this is truly history repeating itself in every one of John's brother's offspring.

But his brother loved him. They had conspired to sign up with the Royal Air Force before conscription occurred to them both. Their plan was to stay together.

Not long after signing up with the RAF, both brothers received conscription papers for the Army.

The rest, as they say, is history.

915792 RAF Volunteer Reserve

John enlisted on the 21st of February 1940 and was initially posted to Bridgnorth.

From his short service history and rapid progress to his overseas posting it seems he fitted like a glove, mechanics were urgently required for the war effort and that fate had already dealt John's final hand.

On the 30th of March he transferred to Yatesbury and wrote to his mother only 24 hours after his arrival. He was impressed with the food and was hopeful of some good sausages, since Harris's were nearby in Wiltshire.

In common with Joe White, John found himself stationed in Lincolnshire from July 1940, manning a radar installation at Stenigot and billeted in private homes in Louth.

Uxbridge followed in November; the formation of 250 MRU (AMES) and their ultimate destination – the Far East.

What a tremendous contrast it was to be posted to Singapore Island in South East Asia. It is conceivable that the men could not believe their luck.

Despite her small size and short history of nationhood, Singapore has a rich heritage. Long before Raffles set foot upon the island, and as early as the 14th century, Singapore was a thriving port.

Legend has it that a prince from the Hindu maritime kingdom centred on Sumatra, seeking independent rule, set out to an island known as Temasek in 1150 AD and as his ship pulled into the natural harbour he spotted a wild cat. From the ship his sighting resembled a red lion. He therefore renamed his new home Singapura, 'City of the Lion'.

Various civilisations jostled for ownership of Singapura over the centuries, until her occupants were overthrown by Siamese armies marching down from Malaysia, a scenario which has a familiar ring to it. However, so total was their destruction, apparently for no purpose, that upon their departure the jungle returned. This of course explains why it was thus found by Sir Thomas Stamford Raffles on the 29th of January, 1819.

Twenty six miles wide and 14 miles long, Raffles favoured the island as suiting the East India Company's trade within the Dutch sphere of influence, because of its strategic position on the southern tip of the Malay peninsula. He'd already tried Penang in Malaysia, and found it to be rife with dysentery, malaria and 'putrid fevers'.

John, a young airman in Wiltshire.

"Mothers Pride". John's mother stands to attention beside her younger son, shortly before he left for Singapore.

John's artistic talents are obvious in this pencil drawing.

54

By the night of Raffles' arrival, Singapura, which was inhabited by a few Malays and their headman, bore a Union Jack, and not much else. She became Singapore, and a free port.

Thomas Raffles did a good job. Despite blinding headaches, and losing three of his four children within his first six months on the island, he drafted a constitution for Singapore, set up a registry of land and laid out streets, settling each race in their own section. He decreed that all men should be equal in the eye of the law and established a college where local languages and tradition were taught. He also collected scientific data on the native plants and wildlife upon the island before losing his fifth child of a few months.

Raffles was named the first president of London Zoo, but on his return to London, the East India Company, whom he had faithfully served for 30 years, had more than a modicum of praise in store for him.

They demanded the reimbursement of £22,000 expenses and advances, much of which had financed the establishment of Singapore on their behalf. Singapore really did mean more to this remarkable man than money, but he didn't have very much longer to concern himself with it. One day before his forty sixth birthday, on the 5th of July 1826, he was found dead at the bottom of a flight of stairs by his wife. He had suffered an epileptic stroke.

His legacy was the establishment of town planning regulations on the island, which resulted in the colony's enviable architectural and urban colonial development.

Four Armenian Brothers, the Sarkies, restored and enlarged a mansion facing the sea on Beach Road. Raffles Hotel opened for business on the 1st of December, 1889, and quickly attracted both British and American elite. This imposing building is now a considerable distance inland.

It must be said that Malaysia and Singapore were populated with large numbers of privileged, naive colonial British at the time of the Japanese invasion. I'm quite sure that among them there were some highly honourable citizens, some of whom lost their lives or their children in the furore which ensued, and I don't mean them any harm. The civilians were as blameless as everybody else, but some civil administration was undoubtedly responsible for compounding the military shortcomings which led to the handing of the area upon a silver platter to the Japanese, together with all her occupants – even those sent to defend her freedom.

Our troops were disliked by the British civilian inhabitants of Singapore Island and Malaysia to the extent that places frequented by them were declared 'out of bounds' to servicemen. Officers excepted, of course.

One of the reasons Lt General Arthur Ernest Percival, the General Officer responsible for commanding in Malaysia, tied his own hands in the proper defence of Singapore, was to placate these ignorant, gin-sling swilling folk and their damnable committees. If it isn't stated now that they contributed, no matter how inadvertently, to the downfall of the Allied troops and the deaths of hundreds of thousands, then it probably never will.

Late on in the campaign, gunners were prevented from cutting down rubber trees to make clear fields of fire, because golf course secretaries insisted there would have to be a meeting of the committee to sanction the digging of trenches on the fairway. I don't see them lining up to take their share of blame with the Japanese.

Paradise Island

I doubt that John ever wanted to leave New Zealand and come back to England, except to be with the rest of his family. His fellow 250 AMES member and good friend, Joe White, actually thought that John was a native New Zealander and was most surprised to learn from me that he was a fellow Englishman.

He was only seven, after all, when the Davey's settled in Napier and since he did not return until he was well into his teens he actually spent more of his life in the Southern Hemisphere than anywhere else. He had no doubts, however, about his roots and Arthur Hargest, "Gramp", was quite well aware that John was a South Londoner, and commented to me on the mysterious lack of accent, which has been passed down the line to my generation.

John's posting to Singapore would have delighted him and all the members of 250 AMES anticipated a fine service life as they boarded the "Empress of Australia", when she set sail from Bootle on the 6th of January 1941. It must have seemed the start of a very great adventure, and in some ways, it was.

The "Empress of Australia" had started her life as the "Prince Eugene", since she was built in Germany. Ironically, she formed part of the reparations payments the Germans were so reluctant to make after World War One, and a luxury cruiser she was not.

Although in 1938 King George VI and Queen Elizabeth sailed aboard her on their first trip to America, 2,600 troops rendered her a little crowded for the passage to Singapore of 250 AMES, and the food was diabolical, the only relatively decent meal being Sunday lunch.

The voyage, of ten weeks duration, is recalled by Bob Bush. "...The large convoy gathered off the south coast of Ireland. At that time our convoys were unable to sail through the Mediterranean, so we sailed down the west coast of Africa, eventually reaching Cape Town.

Here we had the most fantastic reception. The South Africans arrived at the docks in their hundreds, and invited the sailors, soldiers and airmen into their homes. I remember before wishing us 'bon voyage', our host presented us with a huge fruit cake about 2 feet square.

Conditions on the 'Empress of Australia' were very poor indeed....some of us slept in hammocks in E Deck F Section, where the atmosphere could have been cut with a knife. I think it was while we were on the 'E of A' that we crossed the equator and celebrated the ceremony of 'crossing the line'.

In the vineyards of Constantia. John and Joe White (back row left) with Harry Strike (front row left).

57

Above: John sampling grapes en route to Singapore, with Joe White to his right.

*Right: May 1941. In the sea at Singapore Island.
Arthur "Gramp" Hargest on the left, the infamous Harry Strike in the middle and Joe White on the right.*

Below: The unimposing billet to 250 AMES

The superb view from the billet of the Malaysian dwelling, in the grounds of which Jim Hall counted at least ten children.

Shortly after leaving Cape Town, there was a submarine scare and to avoid the danger we sailed up the east coast of Africa to Mombasa, where we stood off the port for two or three days.

Eventually we reached Bombay. Here again there was no shore leave and the troops going to Singapore were taken from the 'E of A' by lighter, to the Cunard liner, the 'Aquitania'. This was a palace compared with the 'E of A'. As there were only about 400 troops, we were able to exercise ourselves. If I remember rightly, four times around the top dock measured one mile.

As we neared our journey's end, we had a wonderful view of the new liner the 'Queen Mary' standing off the island after transporting Australian troops to Singapore. At last we had come to the end of our journey. Leaving the 'Aquitania' we were taken by lorry to R.A.A.F. station Sembawan, where food and conditions were very good. Unfortunately, one of our boys was killed by lightning while swimming, the day after we arrived.

It was not long before we travelled to Changi to our new home at Tanah Besar Road, home for the next nine months."

It was at the end of this informative letter in which Bob had given me everything that I'd asked for, and quite a bit more, that he went on to say, "I sincerely hope these memories of mine will help you to fill a gap in the story of 'Dave'."

That my uncle had such wonderful friends, kind, thoughtful, gentle, considerate, was more than I had ever expected to discover. I began to think then that John had been saying to my subconscious *"find out"*. I had found out, and I realised just how good life in Singapore must have been.

Not only was John a fully qualified radio mechanic; fulfilled in all his working ambitions at that time, he was a free man with no emotional ties at home other than those with his family, with whom he kept in touch very regularly – apart from the odd delay or two. He could be forgiven for this very easily, for after his working shifts he had other duties to attend to.

Apart from being 'orderer in chief' of the 250 AMES canteen, John was very busy playing badminton every day, swimming four or five times a week, generally keeping very fit and playing bridge to boot. Neither post nor pre-war Thornton Heath could provide these facilities which John held so very dear. He took pride in his physique and led the healthy life-style which goes with it.

From March 1941 until February 1942, Tanah Merah Besar (which literally translates from Malay as 'great red earth'), was the billet and 'home' of 250 AMES and was located just south of Changi. Their base, on which John and his unit were dependent for supplies and overall command, was RAF Seletar, further north.

The building which housed 250 AMES was not the most imposing piece of architecture, but it was comfortable and had its own swimming pool and badminton courts. The men also availed themselves of the superb sports facilities of Changi.

Their billet was surrounded by palm trees, so the outlook was certainly appealing. Jim Hall had a wonderful view from his quarters of a typical Malaysian dwelling built of wood and housing a large family. Jim counted no less than ten children over the course of his months there, but believes he lost count in the end.

The pay, especially if you were not obliged to send any to dependents at home, was pretty good. John bought himself a camera and a watch and regularly sent his mother a goodly proportion of his earnings.

On Singapore Island today, the multi-cultural people who inhabit her are concerned that Chinese, Indians and Malaysians should remember and preserve their heritage. They have gone to some lengths to ensure this despite their constant reclamation of land from the sea and need for more buildings.

China Town in Singapore I *would* describe as an impenetrable fortress. The Singapore government would demolish this old ramshackle place over an embarrassing number of dead bodies, or not at all. The Indians, too, have staked their claim to an area which will surely never change. The Malay, with their own country linked to the island by the Causeway, have been the ones to lose out, and their villages have been reclaimed for the building programme which has changed the face of the Island for ever.

So, in deference to the numbers of the Malaysian population and in the true hope that the Malaysian youth will benefit from it (as well as tourists, of course), a 'Malaysian Village' has been constructed towards the north of the island. It is not inhabited and gives a sad impression of the "Marie Celeste", but is otherwise very interesting.

Only when one visits Malaysia does it become apparent that the 'Malaysian Village' was constructed on somewhat idealistic lines, with its trim little decorative touches. The house which Jim saw was the real thing, with a sort of splayed, undecorative, functional look; the 'grounds' in a lived-in mess, and children and chickens everywhere.

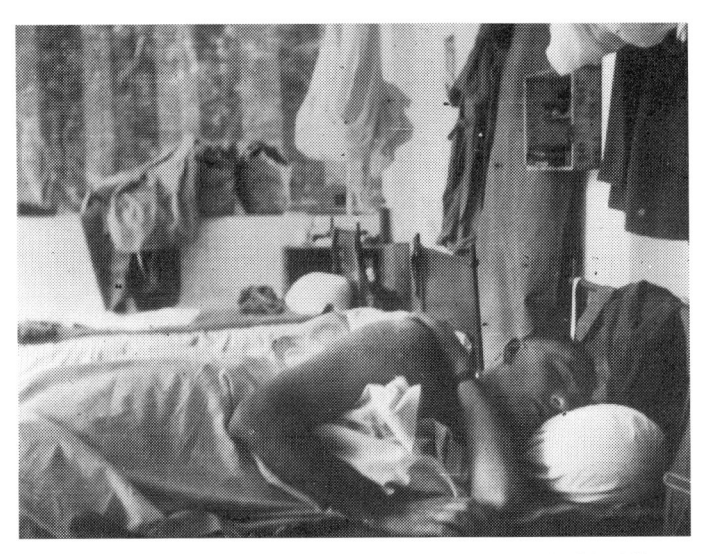

"Gramp" catches forty winks in his quarters. Sergeant Les Bullock's bed is behind him, beyond that is John's. So too is the surrounding clutter. (John's family have maintained this tradition ever since).

John samples a rickshaw.

Jim Hall (right) on the roof of the billet, Changi, with Raymond Frazer.

The beautiful serviceman's resthome in Malacca, where John enjoyed a holiday.

The view of the Malaccan coast taken by John, which was used commercially by the photographer who processed it for him

The reluctant model. Jim Hall had to chase the paperboy to capture him on film.

Trekking through the jungle on Singapore.

250 AMES, Christmas 1941. Unfortunately 915792 Corporal Davey was on duty at the time.

An evening jaunt into Singapore City was a thrice weekly treat, and although John was to all intents and purposes 'teetotal', he could put the stuff away in huge quantities without it having any effect on him whatsoever, according to Arthur "Gramp" Hargest, who in the company of my uncle visited a dancing establishment in Singapore with Sergeant Les Bullock. Since they didn't dance, they decided to 'prop up the bar' instead, and both John and Arthur drank Les under the table, on neat whisky. As Arthur put it, "You may have been told that your uncle didn't drink. Well, he didn't, but he certainly could."

The Radar Operation, 250 AMES was also referred to as MRU (Mobile Radio Unit) and it was those initials which were stamped upon their equipment and supplies. It was perceived that if the men fell into enemy hands then their origins must be disguised – because of the value of their knowledge to the Japanese, for instance – and they were effectively the first line of defence, but then, when you were serving from an 'impenetrable fortress', which Singapore was always so ludicrously considered to be, no one really worried very much about this eventuality.

The climate, of course, was fabulous; despite the sweat rashes and other skin disorders which plagued them, since they were not accustomed to the heat or the humidity of Singapore. Even though the rain fell almost daily, it cooled them, evaporated and then was gone. The sun shone down upon them and their skins tanned.

A boy from the local village would deliver newspapers to 250 AMES from the newsagent. He brought them by bicycle in a sack, just like newspaper boys at home, and evidently, he was considered quite a character. Many of the men wanted to photograph him, because he was a part of their daily lives and added yet more colour to their existence away from home.

He was a most reluctant photographic model, and Jim Hall had to chase him furiously to capture him once on film. During the mens' first Christmas on Singapore, they got the boy drunk and had to carry him, his bicycle and his newspapers back to his village.

The comradeship was second to none. Later on, these men would be bound together forever by a unique kinship born of mutual suffering and survival, but here, in the tranquillity of Tanah Merah Besar, they already enjoyed genuine friendships with one another. Inevitably, some were drawn together in groups. Every man had his special mates. John seems to have been in popular demand. He would be asked to make extra trips into Singapore to keep others company. He would usually then ask Arthur if he would come too.

I can imagine the scenes. Men playing cards and enjoying the canteen facilities. Sports, sleep, reading. The letters from home would have always been special to everyone. Trips into the bright lights of the City. Fascination with the natives. Adventure. They were spared the war at home but not of their own volition. Life was good.

Miraculously, a precious letter home to his parents has survived, and so John, in his own words, is able to describe his life-style in Singapore, his thoughts about home and his aspirations for his future. It is a detailed description of his life with 250 AMES on 'Paradise Island', long-lost Singapore of the 1940s and a piece of history to be cherished forever.

No. 915792 LAC Davey, J.E.,
Radio Station
R.A.F. Seletar
Singapore, S.S.

14/9/41

Dear Mum & Dad,

So far I have letters from you posted on 5/3/41, 3/4/41, 19/5/41 and 16/6/41, from which I should imagine nothing has yet gone astray so far. I believe, as you suspected, however, that one of my letters has been lost although I kept no record of it so I don't know which it was. Still it was bound to be pretty short, eh?

I see by your cable that the allotment has come through alright; you should be getting about 15/2 a week. You might let me know how much you are drawing and when it commenced next time you write please.

Up until today I have not heard from Bill [1] but I see by your last letter that he was writing so it ought to turn up any time now.

I'm pleased to see Bill is in a more enjoyable position than when he was at Compton Bassett although he must have been disappointed that his R.M. course didn't come through straight away. Financially he wouldn't be much different but he would probably find the work more amenable. It shook me to hear he had joined the local conservative club, also that he won the village darts match. He must have improved a lot or else it's a small village!

We (that is Harry and Joe [2] from Louth also) have written to the Le Roux family once or twice since we have been here and received copies of the "photos" they took. The grapes are always worth looking at.

The most plentiful fruits here are bananas at two a penny (to you) also pineapples which you soon tire of. Oranges and apples have to be imported from the U.S.A. or Australia and are, therefore, pretty dear. There are other local fruits which take rather a lot of getting used to however. Coconuts are plentiful enough and we quite often hear them thud down onto the ground. Rather a disturbing sound

[1] John's brother
[2] Harry Strike and Joe White

when you think how often you walk underneath the palms. As a matter of fact that is about the most dangerous thing about this place now, so don't go worrying about me.

What few mosquitoes there are on Singapore Island are not malarial germ carriers even though we use mosquito nets round the beds at night. Snakes are almost non-existent on the Island itself, so on the whole things are as tame as England.

The main grouses about this place are that soon after you get here you almost certainly get "Dobies Itch" which is a raw irritation appearing in the crotch. I had it off and on for a week and luckily have not been bothered since. The only sure way of avoiding it is to well powder that part of the anatomy after washing each day. Another disease is Singapore Ear caused by not drying the ears thoroughly after swimming etc. The usual cure or rather preventative for this is to pour a little methylated spirits in the ear at the end of the swim. Singapore foot is the next in order which is similar to what I had on embarkation leave. Although I have had traces of it on two occasions I soon dispersed it by tying the affected toes up with rags smeared in zinc ointment. Last but not least comes prickly heat which is caused by sweating a lot and which practically everybody has had who does manual work. Even people born here still get it and the only way of keeping it down seems to be plenty of cool showers. After reading this think how lucky you are!

So far I have not met any New Zealanders although there were a lot about at the time I met the Le Roux family. I shall probably write to Jim Butler from here and if he is still in Napier or Wellington I should soon get a reply.

I shouldn't bother to send me any parcels because I can always get most anything here myself. A local paper or two occasionally would be welcome however.

Since I came here I opened a Post Office Savings a/c into which I put all spare cash I can. I shall certainly need all I can lay hands on when this war finishes. Which reminds me I have no record of the No. of my English Post Office a/c so could you let me know, as well as the balance I had there, in case I want to transfer money from the Singapore a/c at any time. The Singapore a/c by the way is run on identical lines to the English.

Thanks for paying my society's fees but it is not my intention to return to accountancy for a livelihood at the end of the ~~ware ware~~ war (got it right that time!). I find my present trade much more suitable and more in my line. As a matter of fact I have thought over the question a lot and am satisfied that it would be foolish to revert to the old job again. For one reason my knowledge now after almost two years is naturally about nil, whereas I have ample opportunity to advance in radio knowledge. I know what I am saying when I tell you that I will do twice as well in my present trade. However, the time I have spent as an accountant has been far from wasted for it is no doubt as good a business experience as you could wish for from an inside point of view.

One job I have here that passes some of the spare time is "orderer-in-chief" of our canteen. As we are a smallish unit we are not supplied with a NAAFI, so we run a canteen among ourselves.

About eight or nine of us take turns at service for a day (the hours are 10–10.20, 12.30–1. and 6–9 at night). The profits are used to buy sports goods and comforts for the unit as a whole – something like a Co-Op.

I see Lewis, Burnell & Webster[1] have moved again and I expect that was because they arranged amalgamation with another firm about the time I left England. I imagine they are still in London somewhere. I heard from Mr. Young before I left and replied to him while at Halton.

So Tom and Edna[2] are raising the population!

The week before last I had seven days leave which I spent with four other fellows up at Malacca, a seaside town about 150 miles up the west coast of Malaya. There is an airmens' rest camp up there which holds twenty airmen at a time. The camp is an ordinary house about three miles from the town itself with some more rooms built on. Each room has two single beds with a chest of drawers etc. and, very important, a large fan suspended from the ceiling. You kicked off the day with tea in bed at 8 o/clock, breakfast at 8.30, tiffin (that is lunch) at 1pm, light tea at 4pm and a four course dinner at 7pm and boy! Some meals too! You come and go as you please and make your own entertainments, they provide plenty of easy cane chairs, books, ping pong table and a badminton court. There are two cinemas in Malacca charging twenty five cents for admission to troops (about 7d.), a dance hall, a fair and some interesting walks. I took quite a lot of photographs up there and also spent a lot of time swimming. There is an excellent sand beach which we unfortunately didn't find until the last day there. All in all it was a reasonable holiday and well worth the visit.

Incidentally I play badminton a lot – practically every day; we have built a couple of courts on the camp. It is very good exercise and what with swimming four or five times a week I am keeping fitter than I was able to in England.

No, I am not faring too badly here, the main disadvantage being lack of home life, there being very few white people here.

Well, I am glad that you are all well, and will close down for the present.

Remember me to all (including Peter and Tiger[3])

Love from
John

P.S. I am sending this by air mail as it is rather a long time since my last letter.

Faithfully reproduced exactly as he wrote it, this single letter from John tells us so much, not only about him and his sense of humour but about service life in the tropics, and the adjustments our men had to make to acclimatise themselves to this beautiful part of the world.

Particularly fascinating are his descriptions of the skin disorders which dogged the men, brought about by excessive sweating in unaccustomed humidity in RAF issue woollen socks. I'm also

[1] John's accountancy firm
[2] John's cousin and his wife
[3] The family budgie and cat respectively

enchanted by the ease with which he was able to so delicately describe to his mother, the symptoms of which many thousands of men were later to nickname "Changi balls" or "rice balls". It is indisputable that malnutrition exacerbated these conditions on the railway, but the servicemen arriving after the capitulation of Singapore became inevitable had no opportunity to acclimatise themselves. Those men already resident had, therefore, some advantage.

I find John's description of the bountiful harvest of Singapore fruit interesting, because now they import literally everything from Malaysia and elsewhere (including their water!). All of their arable land has gone to make way for high-rise flats to house the island's growing population. John would be shocked to see the island now. We went to a fruit wholesalers' there and our guide was stubbornly unmoved by my protestations that his country was once able to grow the exotic fruits he was showing to us, for themselves.

John's assurances to his mother that he is doing the right thing in ditching his accountancy career are touching and easily related to. Parental approval is important to most of us, after all, and John's mother would naturally be anxious that he should pursue a lucrative profession.

His prophetic comments about the most danger he was in being from the falling coconuts and so not to worry about him, and the statement that he would need all the money he could get his hands on when the war was over are poignant in the extreme. So is his reference to tiring of pineapples; such a rich source of vitamins which would later assume great significance.

When John went to Malacca, a trip which he so obviously enjoyed, what was viewed as a rest to his comrades was clearly a holiday for John, who was not accustomed to them. He says he took many photographs, which were either left behind at Tanah Merah Besar or are buried somewhere in Lower Burma, never to be seen again. However, Arthur told me that one of John's photographs of a view of Malacca was used commercially by the photographer who processed them for him.

Joe White completed the picture by handing me the self-same photograph which he had cut from a postcard, bought in Malacca, bearing four photographs of local scenes, my uncle's being one of them.

250 AMES were to enjoy less than a year of their idyllic service life on Singapore Island. The Japanese had plans for South East Asia which mirrored Hitler's in Europe. When John penned his extraordinary letter home to Thornton Heath in September 1941, the German secret police published an order which forbade all Jews over the age of six to appear in public without wearing a yellow star of David, and Hitler was approaching the gates of Moscow. The world was not a nice place to be.

US relations were fast deteriorating with Japan, and perhaps, for John and his comrades, Singapore was the very worst place to be in the whole wide world. But he had no way of knowing what fate had in store for him, or for any of 250 AMES. Within 27 months he would be dead.

The 250 AMES canteen. Bob Bush looks at us from the counter. Arthur Hargest plays bridge with his back to us. Frederick Dobson, "Dobbie", is to Arthur's left.

John enjoys his favourite off-duty pursuit – a game of badminton doubles – with Les Bullock in the foreground.

Above: Orderer in Chief of the 250 AMES canteen, John Davey with Joe White.

Right: John (right) with an unknown mate in Singapore.

68

The fall of Singapore

On December the 7th, 1941 when Japan attacked Pearl Harbour, many of her people were genuinely shocked at the news. Their country was dependent upon America and Britain for her imports of manufacturing machinery, which at that time they did not have the technology to produce themselves.

Why was their country going to war with such powerful nations, especially when Japan's economy would be put at serious risk as a result of such a move? Japan wanted to show the world that she was the most powerful country in the East. She duped her own people and her neighbours into believing that her motive was to ensure that South East Asia as a whole was recognised as a force to be reckoned with, whilst single mindedly pursuing a course of bloodshed, selfishness and greed.

Japan's expansionist plans heralded an advance into China in 1937. In August, Japanese aircraft battered Shanghai with incendiary bombs. According to newspaper reports, Britain seems to have been principally preoccupied with indignation at the injuries sustained by our Ambassador to China at the time.

Two months later, the Duke and Duchess of Windsor made their infamous visit to Germany, where they were personally feted by Adolf Hitler. Only three years hence and following merciless bombing of China by the Japanese, Japan in September 1940 signed a ten year pact with Germany and Italy, converting the Berlin-Rome axis into a triangle for aggression.

The Japanese flouting their power of influence over Asia delighted Hitler with the prospect that America would be engaged in war in the Pacific, thereby less likely to have sufficient resources to interfere with the results of his megalomania in Europe.

Britain at the time was of course in the grip of the Blitz; Germany had invaded France and Winston Churchill uttered the following immortal words:
> "We shall defend our island, whatever the cost may be, we shall fight on the beaches, we shall fight on the landing grounds, we shall fight in the fields and on the streets, we shall fight in the hills: we shall never surrender."

Whilst 250 AMES were en route to Singapore and the war was costing Britain a staggering £11 million a day, the Japanese warned Britain against military movements in South East Asia. We responded by sending more British and Commonwealth reinforcements. Within a few months of their arrival, Japanese troops advanced into Cambodia and Thailand. In the same month Britain and America froze all Japanese assets and Japan retaliated the next day. All the warning signs were there of major trouble ahead.

It is ironic that the bombing of Pearl Harbour by the Japanese finally involved America in World War Two, ultimately scuppering the evil plots of the combined Axis Powers. Mess with dear old Blighty and you get what's coming to you. Mess with Uncle Sam and annihilation is on the cards.

On December the 7th, 1941, Imperial headquarters in Tokyo announced that Japan was at war with the United States and with Britain. Over 2,400 people lost their lives as 360 Japanese warplanes wreaked havoc over Hawaii, the Philippines and Guam and Wake islands in the Pacific. Only 12 days previously, Premier Hideki Tojo had declared that there was nothing to fear in this war. Admiral Nomura and a special envoy from Tokyo were actually engaged in a meeting with the American Secretary of State whilst the attack was taking place. They took Hong Kong 18 days later, on Christmas Day. On the 19th they invaded Malaya (Malaysia).

By the 28th of January they were within 50 miles of Singapore, still being described by the British Media as a fortress. They'd landed in Borneo, the Solomon Islands and New Guinea, and were now threatening Australia only 800 miles away.

About two weeks before the attack on Pearl Harbour and their invasion of Malaya, 250 AMES, John's unit, were alerted and put on 24 hour watch. Jim Hall recalls the details. "On the night watch of 7/8th December 1941, the radar picked up planes at a distance of about 120 miles northeast of Changi, off the coast of Malaya heading south (towards Singapore). In brief, we identified the planes as being 20+ and enemy. The plotting room said they could not be enemy 'because war has not been declared'. They of course were enemy, and the City of Singapore and the naval base were bombed. (Not much point in having early warning equipment if some idiot is going to ignore it!)"

"Changi was the area where the 'powers-that-be' expected the Japs to concentrate their attacks – hence the 6 and 15 inch guns on the northeast coast. It was therefore a dangerous place to be and Seletar insisted that we did not forget to tell them if we were forced to change location – naturally I suppose, as they were responsible for us."

"The daily wagon continued to visit Seletar and, on or about the 6th of February 1942, the wagon arrived at Seletar to find it abandoned – not a soul in sight! They had gone BUT HAD NOT TOLD 250 AMES! The Japs had been on the island for some days but we in 250 AMES had no idea where. The wagon was loaded with rations, mostly tins as emergency supplies, because it was not known where the next lot would come from."

"It was learned later that almost the whole of the RAF had been evacuated to Java, but why the highly secret 250 AMES had been left behind was a mystery – we were then just an early warning system for air-raid alarms! We knew nothing about how the fighting was progressing and had no contact with anyone – we therefore prepared some transport for emergencies."

Singapore burns.

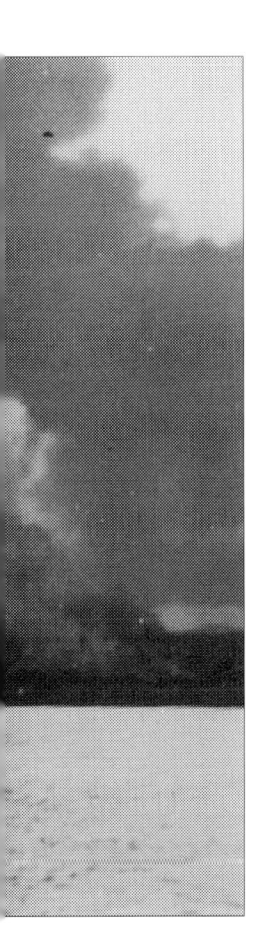

By taking Singapore the Japanese could quash British resistance, our naval base and the army HQ for Malaya. It was fervently believed by the inhabitants of the island and back at home, that the Repulse and the Prince of Wales would see them off by intercepting the Japanese landings in Malaya. Instead they were both sunk with the loss of more than 800 lives.

Sergeant Robert Anderson was in Malaya about three months before the outbreak of the war. When the Japanese invaded, his unit was unable to put up much of a fight because they were continually being ordered to retreat.

His anti-tank gun crew were then ordered to guard the head of the Causeway leading to Singapore, in case the Japanese tried to rush it – and were amongst the very last to leave.

The retreat from Malaya of the British and Australians eventually crossed the Causeway into Singapore. The forces blew up the Causeway behind them, but the 60 yard gap they created was repaired by Japanese engineers on February 11th. We were effectively being backed into a corner.

Once on Singapore, Sergeant Anderson managed to inflict some considerable damage upon the enemy, for which action he received the Military Medal, but the price was the lives of his officer and three of his men, and three and a half years of 'imprisonment' for himself.

The General Officer responsible for commanding in Malaya was Lt General Arthur Ernest Percival. He was nicknamed 'the rabbit'. His defence plan divided the island into three sectors. The Northern sector, defended by the British 18th Division and the Indian 11th and 9th Division were under the command of Lt General Sir Lewis Heath. Major General Gordon Bennett, commander of the Australian Imperial Forces took charge of the Western sector. He had fresh Australian troops and the Indian 44th Infantry Brigade under his command. Lastly, the Southern sector with the 1st and 2nd Malaya Infantry Regiment, the Straits Settlement Volunteer Force, fortress troops and fixed defences were under the charge of Major General Keith Simmons.

Lt General Tomoyuki Yamashita was the Commander of the Japanese 25th Army. He was nicknamed 'the tiger'. His assault plan consisted of a devious ploy to confuse HQ Malaya Command, by creating a diversion in the northeast of the island (on the 7th of February at Pulau Ubin) and then directing heavy artillery bombardment along the entire Northern sector of Singapore to conceal the real landing areas.

Percival had no tanks because London believed them unsuitable for jungle warfare. For the same reason, therefore, he had insufficient anti-tank guns. He had only light gun carriers and approximately 158 obsolete aircraft, namely, ageing 'Brewster Buffalos', because Whitehall

72

considered our air force to be superior to anything the Japanese could muster. Perhaps the Battle of Britain had gone to their heads. There were no Spitfires here. His navy had been decimated by the sinking of the Prince of Wales and the Repulse. Britain had no ships for Singapore which were not engaged elsewhere, and Japan's activities in the Pacific were holding every available US vessel.

Yamashita had 150 tanks and 560 aircraft. He had light steel bicycles and kapok wood boats stolen from the Malayans.

Before the invasion, Percival was warned that he should shore up the Northern defences of the island. All the fixed defences were guarding the South against invasion from the sea. His Chief Engineer, Brigadier Ivan Simpson, for one, was quite convinced that the Japanese would come across the straits from the North. Percival ignored this advice on the grounds that it would alarm both the troops and the civilians on the island if such measures were taken and he was equally convinced that if an assault should come from the North then the four batteries of 6 and 15 inch guns located in the North East would see them off. It was never even contemplated that the Japanese would attempt an attack from the peninsula where they would be confronted by jungle.

The feint attack on Pulau Ubin after nightfall on the 7th of February was met with minimum resistance. Large troop movements had been sighted in the rubber plantations across Jahore but Percival was uninformed about this until only hours beforehand.

Communications were then destroyed by bombs dropped upon military headquarters in the Western sector, as intensive firing by Japanese artillery continued. On the night of the 8th of February they infiltrated the North West coast line, and although the Australians put up a good fight, they were outnumbered, ran out of ammunition and were ultimately beaten by the breakdown of communication with their command.

The Japanese fired a red starshell to signify their landing and later a white starshell burst over the Straits to confirm their successful infiltration. They forced the withdrawal of the defence line covering the Northern approaches to Tengah Airfield, largely with air bombardment, in the afternoon of the 9th of February.

In the pre-dawn darkness of the 10th of February, Yamashita first set foot upon Singapore Island; the bastion of the British Empire East of Suez. He suffered major losses that day at the Kranji River in the North West when flaming oil gushed into the water, where his troops were under-cover. Due south from here was the Jurong River and loss of areas on the 'line' between the two would give the Japanese access to Singapore City. Percival thus ordered reinforcements, an Australian brigade, to the Bukit Panjang–Keat Hong Road junction to the right of the line.

Percival sensibly had a reserve plan up his sleeve. His last stand, if all else failed, was to hold a perimeter covering Kallang Airfield. These instructions were issued in secret to his generals but for some unknown reason were misunderstood. The troops defending the Kranji–Jurong Line were withdrawn to the perimeter position, leaving the way clear for the Japanese advance. Unbelievably, another misunderstanding of Percival's instructions led to the withdrawal of troops from the Causeway, enabling the Japanese to proceed inland from the North.

Poor John. Poor everybody. What an unmitigated disaster. Enter the Japanese tanks.

Yamashita wanted Singapore on the 11th of February as a tribute to the anniversary of the Emperor Jimmu. As their ammunition was now running low, he had letters dropped over Percival's HQ, urging him to throw in the towel. Percival moved to his final protective perimeter, 28 miles long. Yamashita moved to the Ford Motor Factory.

It goes without saying that our defending forces were tired and demoralised. Civilian casualties were mounting and Percival was urged to surrender. He would not.

Meanwhile, back at 250 AMES, John and his colleagues received their belated 'instructions' to evacuate. Jim Hall continues with the story:

"On Friday the 13th of February an army despatch rider came speeding into the unit, didn't stop, circled and shouted words to the effect that we should leave immediately because the Japs were 'just around the f...... corner.'"

"The Radar Units – transmitters and receivers – were flooded with petrol and hand grenades thrown in. The petrol dump was also fired, as was the office and accommodation."

"Off we went on the prepared transport. Someone asked where we were going and it was decided that we should try and reach the docks about 16–18 miles away on the basis that what was good enough for the remainder of the RAF was good enough for us."

"We eventually reached the dock gates which were locked and guarded by Military Police. It was explained who we were and what had happened and we were accused of being army deserters dressed in stolen RAF uniforms. Eventually we were allowed through the gates and to board the 'Tien Kwan' which sailed at sunset (Friday 13th). Up to this stage we had been fortunate to survive mortar attacks, several bombing raids and falling masonry, etc. However, this good luck abandoned us at sunrise the next morning when we were spotted by a 'recce' plane and bombed and machine-gunned near the uninhabited island of Pompong and suffered our first casualties of four killed and several wounded. However, the losses whilst in the prison camps were very much higher".

At Pasir Panjang Ridge the 1st and 2nd Battalion Malay Regiment waged a 48 hour stand against the Japanese to no avail. The Japanese wreaked their revenge on the patients and staff of Alexandra Hospital, bayonetting 200 innocent victims to death on the 14th of February.

On Sunday the 15th of February 1942, Lt. General Arthur Ernest Percival still had plans for continued fighting, but he agreed to meet with Yamashita under a flag of truce at the Ford Motor Factory on the Bukit Timah Hill. The water supply was failing; epidemics would arise from its loss just as surely as night follows day. Most supply depots were in Japanese hands. The prognosis was not too good.

The final irony of the situation was that Yamashita's casualties had rendered his troops outnumbered three to one. They too were tired and with severely depleted ammunition he feared that he would have to withdraw to Malaya to await fresh supplies and reinforcements of men.

He bluffed. He threatened to launch an all-out assault that night. Percival, who had prevaricated, agreed to unconditional surrender. Thus fell Singapore Island to the Japanese.

The Japanese triumphed through cunning, subterfuge and stealth. Our defeat seems to have been caused by misunderstanding, lack of co-ordination and an amalgamation of seemingly endless strategic cock-ups, unparalleled in the entire history of the British Empire.

Cutting off the water supply would hasten the British surrender. Yamashita lost no time in targeting the Seletar, Peirce and MacRitchie reservoirs.

The Japanese had defeated the British in only ten weeks. Our troops, some of whom had been sent as lambs to the slaughter only days before the fall of the island, were not equipped for fighting in the jungle or accustomed to the conditions. They were frequently at the receiving end of the consequences of poor leadership.

These men had been badly used but would have gone on as long as they were able to do so in order to prevent defeat. But capitulation was thrust upon them, and I can only try and imagine their feelings as they faced the unknown result of surrender to the Japanese.

What was going through John's mind and those of his comrades when they discovered the betrayal of the RAF in leaving them behind without a word and in the dark? 250 AMES were not trained fighters, they were radio operators. They had no other alternative than to take their chances with escape and their terror of what might lay ahead throughout their desperate passage is unthinkable. The expressions on the men's faces, captured forever on film to haunt us all portray their hopelessness, as they tried to reach Sumatra in one piece, and before it was too late.

Badly let down were the Chinese, Malay and Indian inhabitants of Singapore Island. These civilians had trusted us to protect them. They had believed that the British would look after them, yet they found themselves deserted and at the mercy of the Japanese. With no food or water and leaving looted or burning homes, they fled into the chaos of the aftermath of surrender and a great many of them, men, women and children, were to lose their lives.

All pawns. Victims every one. Even Percival was a hostage to the futility of war, and to lay all of the blame at this man's door simply deepens the wound. It doesn't solve anything and it perpetuates the injustices resulting from a conspiracy of fatalistic evil.

Among the victims were many heroes. Individuals put their own skin second in order to help and to save others. Selfishness reared its ugly head, of course, but there were many glorious incidences of overt consideration for their fellows taking priority over self preservation.

The cost of the war in Europe and the resources which it deployed meant that Britain simply wasn't in a position to provide the necessary weight in the Far East to prevent the invasion of the Japanese. This was compounded by a foolish assumption; an arrogance, that we were so superior to the Japanese that whatever they did would be inadequate, and that we could easily beat them. Combine this with the ridiculous notion that Singapore was impenetrable and you have the perfect recipe for total disaster.

Churchill described the loss of the fortress (as the media were *still* calling it) as a heavy and far reaching military defeat. He went on to say, "here is the moment to display that calm and poise, combined with grim determination, which not so very long ago brought us out of the very jaws of death." Well, what *could* he say; but if I close my eyes and concentrate I can hear the sound of the bombs dropping on Singapore. I can smell the burning and feel the heat of the infernos. I can hear the screams of the civilians and the shouts of our poor men. And in my heart I can sense the panic and the desperation. "Got to get out", "must survive", "cannot fall into the hands of these yelling, bayonetting bastards". "I want to go home". I can taste my uncle's fear.

But it got worse. Oh, my dear God it got so much worse, and most of those who did get home had to survive three and a half years of purgatory before they did so.

At home, genuine shock and horror at the fall of Singapore perpetrated, and the feelings of the families of the men involved were desperate. News was not coming through with precise details; no one knew who was already dead and who would go on to suffer gross deprivation at the hands of their captors. No one at home knew what this would entail. mothers, fathers, wives, fiances, girlfriends, brothers, sisters, grandparents, aunts and uncles could only hold their breath and pray. The disconcerting news that John was 'missing believed POW' eventually reached Norbury Avenue. John's mother frequently dreamt about her son and pictured him with a bandaged head, convinced that he was injured.

A valiant drive on behalf of the British Red Cross and St.John's Ambulance appealed for the nation's help in providing for prisoners of war. Posters of a rather healthy looking, if desperate soldier behind barbed wire, clutching an open parcel of goodies to his bosom was captioned, 'a bit of home'. Such parcels did infiltrate the Far East during World War Two, but those which were not kept by the Japanese for their own use were stockpiled in their thousands. Photographic evidence of this exists until this day and is conclusive proof of the barbarism of the Japanese in this most damning period of the history of their culture.

If we can face up to failure and the incompetence which cost the British Singapore, why cannot the Japanese concede their inhumane past, and teach it to their children so that the lessons may be learned? Why, if Germany has had her nose justifiably rubbed into the atrocities of the Holocaust cannot the Japanese accept her past miscreants and acknowledge them properly?

Atrocities have been committed by every nation upon the earth at one time or another. How are we to grow away from the evils and futility of warfare unless we confront, discuss and consider the motivation and detail of man's aggression and inhumanity? Should we interpret such a bald refusal to own up as shame? Or does it imply a threat that leopards do not change their spots and look to the East for future conflict? Are her people really so different from us in the Western world?

In an attempt to redress the balance, I perceive that all of our preoccupation with our warfaring history tends to concentrate upon victory, and we do not always give just credit to our allies and their undeniable contribution, which in many instances will have tipped the scales just far enough to have made all the difference to the final outcome. Perhaps we should look also at our weaknesses and our inadequacy. No one is invincible. Even Nelson, in his inimitable style as active leader of his men was a sitting target for the French sniper aboard the Redoubtable as he stood upon the quarter deck of HMS Victory, bedecked with all his tell-tale medals.

No one could persuade him to take them off, or to retreat to a safer place below decks. He did his duty. He stood proudly among his men to oversee his strategic victory, but was mortally wounded in the process. We have many heroes, but we've lost an awful lot of them in their prime.

Chapter 6

Not only did allied troops retreat into Singapore across the Causeway for their final stand against the Japanese. The families of business men, planters and mining engineers who were the British community in Malaya, poured into Singapore in their thousands in the weeks before the capitulation. They had of course left their property and most of their belongings behind them.

Colonel Alan Ferguson Warren of the Royal Marines was a Dunkirk veteran who led a secret unit which co-ordinated with the Dutch to transport escapees across to Sumatra. The port of Padang, the most densely inhabited town on the West coast of Sumatra, was their target, from where ships would take them to Java.

The problem was that Colonel Warren's unit was so secret that not everybody knew about it, or the evacuation plan. The speed with which the Japanese infiltrated made it impossible for Colonel Warren to make detailed arrangements, or to communicate them adequately to all concerned. This is why the evacuation, which saved many thousands of lives, was too little, too late for 250 AMES and many others besides.

To understand the enormity of the task and the difficulties which prevailed, you have to imagine the total chaos which reigned upon the island at the time, and the panic, which among human beings can be very counter-productive. It must also be understood that no one wanted to fall into Japanese hands, particularly if their valiant efforts to defeat the enemy were being scuppered by strategic disaster, beyond their own control.

The exodus in which 250 AMES found themselves a part, more by luck than through any kind of instruction, was to be the very last to leave the island. After this, everyone was on their own. The criteria for selection was men who had skills useful to any future war effort and nurses and medical staff. No civilians. Not even the old, the sick or the women.

Assorted craft of all descriptions, 44 in all, would berth approximately 3,000 people. The army were allocated 1,800 places including 100 for the Australian Division. The remainder were to go to naval technicians, senior officers and the remaining RAF personnel. 250 AMES at the time were now behind enemy lines and still operational. The Asian crews of the local vessels purloined for escape were discharged on orders from the Royal Navy.

The severely limited capacity of these vessels for evacuation purposes necessitated the dire secrecy of the operation, but the 'chosen ones' were supposed to report to Clifford Pier by 4pm on Friday the 13th of February. Whilst the evacuation planning meeting was still taking place at lunchtime, 250 AMES remained operational and uninformed, 18 miles away at Changi Point.

John and his mates were very fortunate to eventually find themselves aboard the 'Tien Kwan' sailing in the opposite direction to Keppel Harbour. She was a flat-bottomed riverboat and in common with another 41 of the 44 evacuation vessels, she was sunk by the Japanese. She was hit on the stern by a bomb and heavily machine gunned. 250 AMES lost four men during this attack, two of them whilst manning a machine gun mounted on the bridge (Corporal Stewart Pyke and LAC Eric Lewis), and Reginald 'Ginger' Watkinson who had volunteered for engine room duty. The fourth, whose name is unknown to me, was last seen holding onto the anchor chain minus one leg. Others were killed in the water whilst trying to get ashore on Pompong Island.

Part of the master plan of the evacuation was, of course, to ensure that there were adequate food supplies en route. This couldn't have been easy when survivors of sunk vessels were making for the nearest dry land and no one could be sure when replacement vessels would arrive to resume the inhabitants' passage.

Jim Hall has described Pompong as the only island in South East Asia without a coconut. Palm trees? Nil. It was three to four days before a water supply was found by a desperate dog, and low rations meant there was insufficient to boil a handful each of rice. There have been rumours of biscuits and even corned beef being available on Pompong, but these must have long since been eaten by the time John and the rest of 250 AMES clambered ashore.

Apart from a single strip of beach, Pompong's shoreline consists of razor-edged rock or spiky coral surrounded by a powerful current. Around this lapped the oil from sunken vessels. About two miles in circumference and quite round, the island is entirely covered by lofty trees, and inedible jungle.

Civilians *had* made their way onto Pompong; there were about 250 scantily clad women and children. The men behaved like perfect gentlemen and bequeathed items of their own limited clothing. Joe White gallantly provided a near-naked nursing sister with his shirt.

Bodies and limbs were occasionally washed up on the shore, and these were buried in the sand. Those casualties who died amid the rocky territory of the hilltop 'hospital', however, were not.

After six days, when the food situation was extremely serious, a small naval patrol vessel, the HMS Tanjong Pinang, reopened the route to freedom for about 170 women, children and a few very badly wounded men. No one would deny these poor innocents a passage out of hell, but since no civilians were meant to have participated in this evacuation phase – an appallingly inhumane decision but a sound military one nonetheless – you can actually understand the reasoning behind it. The men had already been on the island for six days with hardly any food. The priority was to get to Padang whilst it remained an open town, and there were still ships coming into dock to take them safely to India. More delay cost a lot more than freedom.

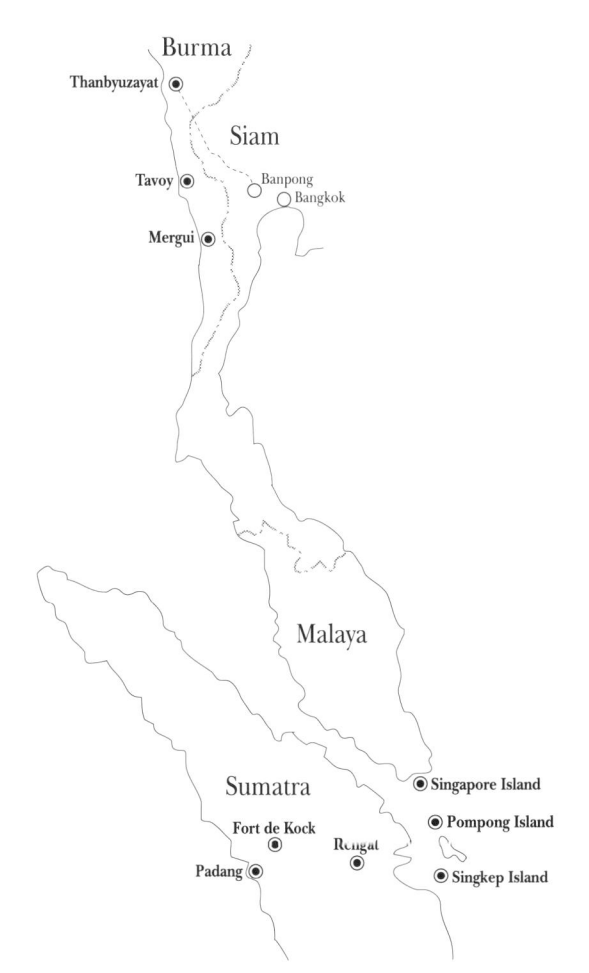

From the bridge of the 'Tien Kwan', which took John and 250 AMES to temporary safety.

Pompong Island viewed from the 'Tien Kwan'.

The train journey to Padang, and capture by the Japanese.

80

The skipper of HMS Tanjong Pinang, around a 133 ton diesel vessel with very poor defences, was a New Zealander, Lt Commander Shaw. He was ready to go to Australia, if necessary and believed that his fuel stocks and canned supplies were sufficient to take him anywhere.

The general policy of the evacuation plan was to lie low and disguise your vessel during the daytime and to make whatever headway you could by night, for obvious reasons with Japanese bombers dominating the skies. Shaw decided to press on regardless; not an entirely bad course of action in the circumstances, and he made good progress. Shaw had got to Sumatra, before being sent back to Pompong Island. He already had a great many wounded on board. It was 3am when the Tanjong Pinang left Pompong on her last voyage.

Shaw headed for Batavia, with no way of knowing that Palembang on the way had fallen. Searchlights lit up her decks and two shells hit the ship. The hold took the full brunt of one of them; she listed and then turned right over. Only those who had 'gone to bed' in their life-jackets stood much chance. The sick, injured and dying were immediately despatched into the sea.

The nursing sisters swam around in the dark amongst the floating bodies and managed to rescue 14 people, including six children, two of whom were under one year old.
Lt Commander Shaw sailed off into the night on board a badly leaking lifeboat to get help. He was never seen again.

Left helpless on a raft in the tropical sun, by the 19th of February the survivors were whittled down to two. They caught a couple of pieces of driftwood and started to paddle with them, but Mrs Barnett lost hers and disappeared into the sea in pursuit of it.

The one remaining lady was Dame Margot Turner, who was rescued, unfortunately by the Japanese. She suffered her own three and a half years of hell in captivity.

Back on Pompong, John and the others had spent approximately eight days on the island before three tonkins arrived, probably alerted by Malay fishermen who days earlier had taken 'Tubby' James and Corporal Bill Hughes to safety. The latter two members of 250 AMES has shrapnel wounds and were lucky enough, eventually, to reach Ceylon. The remaining survivors were off Pompong at last and on their way to Singkep.

This island had coconuts, and more rice. 250 AMES were a little alarmed to be greeted by a Dutch soldier wearing a white neckerchief, but when asked if Japs were on the island he replied that they were not. Offers of assistance were not forthcoming. You did not have to have a limb hanging off to require first aid.

I asked Arthur Hargest if it was a case of every man for himself, during the evacuation as well as later, when their evacuation experience would seem like a picnic by comparison. He replied that it was much more a case of 'every man for his small group'. This, plainly, is the secret of survival.

Because of the three tonkins, which were miniature junks, the men were temporarily split up and arrived at Singkep at intervals where they were billeted in the new native quarters of a tin mine. More precious days were lost here waiting for further transport, but in the words of Jim Hall, a Chinese gentleman was 'persuaded' to take them in his junk to the mouth of the crocodile infested Indragiri River.

Here, as Arthur recalls, the vessel broke down and the men put up at a trading post until they were able to make their way to a rubber factory on the river where there was 'not much else'. Arthur is right. On old maps of the area this location is marked 'factory'. There *is* nothing else. But at least they'd made it to Sumatra.

The next port of call was Rengat. Somewhere, around this time, Jim Hall celebrated his 21st birthday on the 6th of March with the sole consumption of a small, fried banana – which made him sick.

250 AMES were now able to make their way to Padang by lorry and then by train, crossing the mountains to the west of Sumatra and arriving at the port, where only days beforehand, ships refuelling there had been able to take evacuees to freedom. But on the 8th of March Java capitulated and by April the 5th the Japanese were bombing Ceylon. Although they were not able to repeat their Pearl Harbour decimation, because British defences at Colombo were prepared for their arrival, the Japanese were acknowledged to have a naval force in the Indian Ocean.

There were no ships for 250 AMES. There was no passage to freedom. The Dutch, who had declared Padang a free town in the hope that they may have negotiated better surrender terms, disarmed the arriving and stranded men. There were local vessels to hand in this busy port and the chance to make one last desperate run for it must have been overwhelming. I'm not aware that anybody did, or, had they done so, how far they would have got. There was basically nowhere to run and nowhere to hide. There were hundreds of men in the same position, from all three services.

Colonel Warren, who as the most senior British Officer in Padang, was left in no doubt by the Dutch that he was considered responsible for the actions of all the men in question, was expected to ensure that none of the native boats were stolen. He found himself in a very awkward position, therefore, since the Dutch Military Commander was by this time preoccupied with delicate negotiations with the Japanese as he prepared to hand them the town, on orders from somewhere above.

Above: An early casualty. The grave of Corporal Fairbrass on Pompong Island.

Left: The despair which was Pompong and escape.

Left: Evacuees leave Pompong at last, in the cramped hold of a junk.

Above: Sinkep Island.

Above left: Priji Raja, at the mouth of the Indragiri River.

Left: Rengat.

The British Sumatra Battalion

The British Camp Commandant of the men from all three services who found themselves prisoners of war of the Japanese at Padang, was Captain Morley RA. He was required to select 500 men (including 20 officers), to leave for an 'unknown destination'.

They were a mixed bunch if ever there was one, made up as follows:

187 Royal Artillery
 88 RAF
 79 Royal Navy
  5 RAOC
 13 Royal Engineers
 24 Royal Corp of Signals
 17 RASC
 10 Royal Norfolk Regiment
  3 Royal Marines
  6 Cambridgeshire Regiment
  5 Leicesters
  4 Sherwood Foresters
  1 Gordon Highlander
  1 Northumberland Fusilier
  6 Federated Malay Straits Volunteers
  2 Searchlight Regiment
  6 East Surrey Regiment
 15 18th Division Recce Corp
  7 Hong Kong and Shanghai Volunteers
  6 Argyll and Sutherland Highlanders
  2 Loyal Regiment
  2 Beds and Herts Regiment
  6 General Services

and Colonel Sir Albert Coates AIF as MO.

For some reason known only to himself, Captain Morley decided to include in this party, anyone who had shown signs of being a trouble-maker in his captivity to date.

There were common denominators which would link men who were previously unknown to each other (all the Geordies found each other for a start), but otherwise there was nothing to unite them other than their common fate.

By now, there was not a great deal of natural respect being felt by any man towards the officers of the services, let alone those of an unknown unit. They had, after all, grounds for cynicism towards command which was synonymous with mismanagement in their view. One of the officers was the Malay hangman, who although not accountable for the combined disasters leading to the sorry situation in which the men now found themselves, was probably not best equipped to lead them either.

Desmond Pretyman Apthorp (alias Captain Dudley Apthorp) was appointed to take the immense responsibility upon his shoulders at the tender age of 29, to lead them, discipline them and to ensure their survival, against appalling odds.

That so many did survive was testimony to the efforts of this man and he could not possibly have saved any more. That disease, overwork, inhumane treatment and malnourishment did take their toll on his men was in no way the fault of Captain Dudley Apthorp.

In Thailand the British casualties were far worse, and apart from the numbers being greater at this end of the line, the men did not have the stability of their units or the benefit of adequate or sometimes any command. Something as simple as boiling – water, cooking and eating utensils – was a matter of life and death. Keeping your dignity was paramount to survival and without the authority of a clean-shaven, fully uniformed and thoroughly 'proper officer', the mental stress of disorder, on top of everything else, was more than enough to send men to their graves.

No matter how jaundiced the men had become towards authority, or how much worse things were to become for them, they seem unstinting in their praise towards the man who led them through hell.

Their journey together began on May the 9th, 1942 when they left Padang by train and road bound for Medan on the north coast of Sumatra. In this same month, 'A Force', a group of several thousand Australians, left their imprisonment at Changi in Singapore, also bound for Burma.

It was in Medan that the extent of Japanese brutality was brought home to everyone. A local was caught thieving and was made to sit at a table, to which both his hands were bayonetted.

The Japanese were determined the POW officers would manage their prisoners in terms of administration, the distribution of rations, medical attention and so on. This may not have seemed ideal to the officers but must have been better for the men and it reduced the number of guards required to oversee them. Despite ludicrously inadequate resources it did at least preserve some independence.

86

Bob Bush.

Jim Hall.

Joe White.

Arthur Hargest.

Charles Peall.

Peter Dunstan.

My father, William Francis Davey and his own RAF unit, 45 MSU (Mobile Signals Unit) – he is the very handsome one in the front middle. He was not, of course, a FEPOW, and served in Europe. I wonder, though, what might have occurred if he had signed up together with John as planned.

88

The men's uniforms were hopelessly depleted and possessions were virtually nil. Apart from a few rough necks, most of the men were decent enough, and Dudley was quite determined to maintain law and order.

Their first stop, after a day's rail journey, was Fort de Kock, where the night was spent in an empty convent. The next day they set off in lorries at great speed for Hota Nopan. Sweat rash and hunger dogged this phase of their journey, and they could not have been very happy to see native children waving paper Japanese flags in all the villages they passed through.

After a night in a disused school, the same trucks with Japanese at the wheel, tackled the mountain roads which led them to a railed market place at Tarotoeng. The distribution of two very small 'loaves' per man in the dark led to the baddies getting four and others none. Trading went on through the railings with the locals and some remaining shirts and shorts were exchanged for cash.

On the 12th of May they arrived at the port of Belawin Deli, where they shared a camp with Dutch civilians. Barbed wire was meant to keep them apart, but according to Dudley, the Dutch were very generous with their supplies and shared what they had with the Battalion.

Three days later, they found themselves aboard the 'England Maru', a small British steamer built in 1898. Some of 'A Force' were already on board, and the most appallingly cramped voyage lay ahead for them all.

Dysentery had already become a problem for many, and since the 'toilet' was a wooden cradle suspended over the side by ropes and seating only two at a time, the discomforts were obvious. The hold was hot and airless and the numbers of passengers rendered the vessel highly reminiscent of an African slave ship. She sailed in convoy with the rest of the Australian 'A Force' and did not arrive in Mergui until the 25th of May.

Following a one mile march all 1,500 men squeezed into the National High School for the night, which was intensely humid and wet, since the monsoons were under way.

Dudley Apthorp's pride and his men's resolve came into their own in the light of the deprivation of the British compared with their Australian counterparts. The Australians were well dressed in their uniforms. Many of Dudley's men were presumably down to their underpants. But the former had been sent to and from Singapore equipped in their units, in which they had remained. The same could not be said of anyone in the British Sumatra Battalion. 250 AMES, for example, had not had the opportunity to collect from their billet, anything which they did not have upon them at the time of their departure. Even had they done so, it is unlikely that they would have been much better equipped following their evacuation adventures.

Dudley's contempt for the Japanese was infamous, and he was not noticeably pro Australian or Dutch either, since he felt that there was too much kowtowing going on in these quarters. He was determined that he and his men would get up as many Japanese nostrils as possible.

The men, however, made many friends with individuals from all nationalities. John probably had a special affinity with Australians because of his love of New Zealand, and to an Aussie, if you were a pommie bastard you were just fine. If you were a bastard pommie that was another thing altogether. Jim Hall borrowed a cape from an Australian on camp duties, who also gave him a 'digger' hat. They were all in it together – up to their necks.

Dudley helped mould his group into one of outstanding toughness and character and, although sometimes viewed as trouble-makers by the others, the Battalion took pride in defying the Japanese at every opportunity. He frequently took beatings on his own account and for his men, which although I have previously mentioned in this book is worth repeating. He protected his sick and improved conditions for the whole of the Battalion whenever possible. No wonder he earned the accolade of being by far the bravest man ever known by fellow officers.

Dysentery struck again at Mergui. Many men were critically ill after their voyage upon the 'England Maru'. Colonel Sir Albert Coates, AIF, lost no time in directing the medical facility in a part of Mergui Hospital, which had been set aside for POWs. It was at this time that rice for every meal was served to the men and, at first, it caused severe constipation; 20 days was the average – longer for some unfortunates. Dysentery followed.

Within a month, 12 members of the Battalion were already buried in the local cemetery, one of whom hailed from 250 AMES, Corporal W R Hill. Bill Hill was built like a brick outhouse and was the very last person on whom any RAF man would have placed a bet for early demise.

LAC Harry Courts was luckier. He survived a dangerous bout of dysentery at this early stage of captivity and lived to tell the tale. When Harry came around after a period of unconsciousness, he asked Dudley for some clothes when he visited the hospital, since he had woken up in his 'birthday suit'. Harry was apart from John and the remainder of 250 AMES within the Battalion, who were building runways at Mergui airfield, and did not know that there was no clothes issue. Dear Dudley still managed to find him a pair of shorts – with 25 patches, a length of green curtaining and a hub cap. The latter item was a recognised substitute for a plate, from which Harry ate his paltry meals for three and a half years.

The food situation was awful at Mergui, and when Dudley and his Australian counterpart asked the Japanese for meat, vegetables and salt they were told 'no', 'boil the grass' and 'take your salt from the sea', respectively.

Unfortunately the sea was also filled with Burmese excreta, dead cattle, dogs and pigs for some reason, but this was their water source for cooking. A bonus in collecting this evil brew was that kind Burmese dropped little gifts of food into the containers, wrapped in banana leaves.

The bells and the drums of Burmese temples rang out in this place. Sounds which I will hear during my pilgrimage in November 1994 and will then haunt me as they would have John. They were of course a little trying to Westerners, especially in these dreadful circumstances, but the priests sometimes gave round tins of cigarettes to the men, which were very gratefully received.

Rats, scorpions, millipedes, huge spiders and lizards were fellow residents, but eventually the Japanese succumbed to pressure from both Dudley and Colonel Coates (a very empathetic Australian ally of the Battalion) and a new camp was built for them near the jail which had previously been their 'home'.

The Japanese guards who supervised the work of the Battalion on the new runways at Mergui airfield were in short supply. They therefore had to move from one working party to another and the code 'red light' meant that a guard was coming and 'green light' that he'd gone and everyone could stop working. When a guard approached them shouting 'red light' himself, he aptly demonstrated that he was a fellow human being with a sense of humour.

They had, however, also recruited local women to break up large stones, many of whom were in assorted stages of pregnancy or carrying their babies with them as they worked.

On the 10th of August it was apparently time to move on, although once again no one knew where they were headed because they were never told. Their march to the docks was accompanied by the Australian band playing 'Good old Sussex by the Sea', and they were then crammed onto the 'Tatu Maru' in the pouring rain.

Although they sailed for only a day and found themselves in Tavoy, they were transferred to the holds of two lighters for ten hours, where there was insufficient room to do anything but sit with their knees bent in the pitch darkness. It was then a great relief to get out, march to the outskirts of the town and commence work at another aerodrome.

The food situation and general conditions were much the same as in Mergui, except 'stray' cattle kept appearing in the camp, courtesy of pro-British Burmese who were prepared to endanger their own lives in order to help our men.

There was also a working party for the town and those lucky enough to get on it were apparently cashing cheques and having their lunch in cafes. All my friends from 250 AMES can recall is the building of runways.

The death rate improved at Tavoy, the principal killers being amoebic dysentery and serious tropical ulcers. Colonel Coates was now resident at the Tavoy Hospital and performing amputations without the use of drugs or dressings even then.

This miracle-worker was well loved by the men, each one of whom seems to have been addressed as 'laddie' by Colonel Coates. Later on in the camps on the line he would march through the tropical ulcer hut with a pair of steel scissors in his hand. If he came across something he didn't like the look of he would stop and say "that toe's doing you no good, laddie. I think it had better come off", and so it would, there and then.

It was whilst in Tavoy that Sergeant Les Bullock requested permission to volunteer his services to the Japanese, to repair a British wireless receiver they had found at the home of a civilian. His true purpose was to both sabotage it by reducing its effectiveness and to purloin parts for his own use in illicit radio construction later on. Captain Apthorp recommended him for an RAF decoration in recognition of his construction and operation of a hidden radio set from December 1942 until January 1944. He was acting Sgt Major to 'a company of POWs composed of RAF personnel', who included John Davey and the rest of 250 AMES.

92

The Burma-Siam Railway

Thanbyuzayat was reached by the British Sumatra Battalion on the 23rd of October 1942 via Moulmein, just as it is today. The 40 mile distance between the two was covered by rickety train.

The inhabitants of Moulmein had treated the men very differently to any other locals they had encountered to date, greeting them with gifts of food, tobacco and cheroots. Some women cried whilst others presented them with trays of home-baked biscuits and cakes. They were literally swamped with generosity and kindness.

During the one night spent at Moulmein jail, the men found a collection of old enamel buckets. They had not been cleaned from their previous use, which need not be described, but Jim Hall purloined one and it became a cherished container for his few belongings as he made his way from camp to camp in the years of captivity which lay ahead.

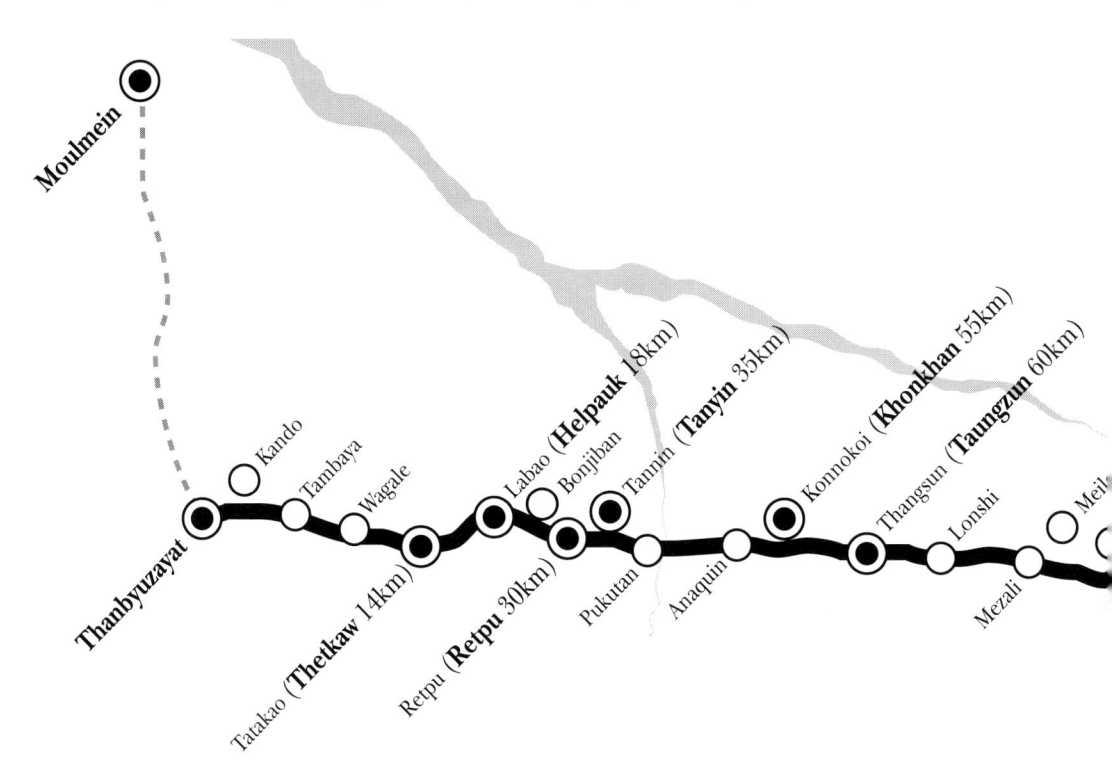

Map of the Burma-Siam Railway interpreted and based on original Japanese Army map by Australian POW's.

I know now what my uncle saw. He saw Kipling's old Moulmein pagoda in all its golden glory. In different circumstances he could have appreciated being one of the few visitors to this wonderful country, enjoying the unique friendliness and hospitality of its peace-loving people. I'm convinced that John would have been receptive to all of this, regardless. His sense of adventure would not have permitted him to do otherwise.

Thanbyuzayat is a typical little Burmese village, bustling with daily life. Pronounced 'Than-byou-zay-at', it took its name from the grey and white painted resting place built by Buddhists long, long ago for the convenience of passing travellers. The 'zayat' here has a wooden floor and a corrugated 'tin' ('Than Byu') roof. Hence this mysterious, magical, very appropriate and commonly un-pronounceable name.

A railway line already linked Thanbyuzayat with Ye, further south. It is still there. The plan of the Japanese was to link it with Bangkok in Thailand, opening up a supply route for their troops in Burma which would avoid the use of the sea, upon which they were vulnerable to Allied attacks. It was as simple as that.

Even Japanese engineers had said that it could not be done, because much of the terrain which separated the two points was composed of dense jungle and mountainous territory. The Japanese were, however, determined that it would be built and frankly they did not care what it cost in terms of human life of their captives. They had made this crystal clear to their 60,000 allied prisoners in all their assorted groups, with expressions ranging from "there will be great

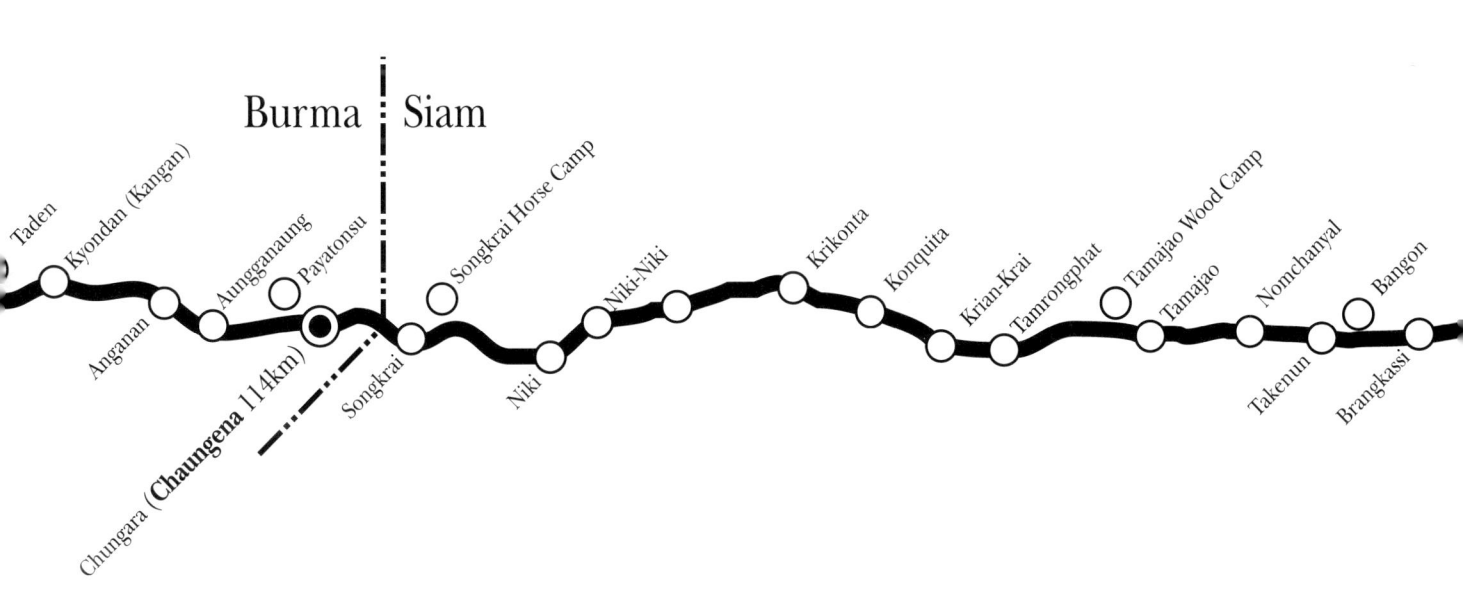

loss of life, Nippon very sorry", to "you are remnants of a decadent white race and fragments of a rabble army. This railway will go through even if your bodies are to be used as sleepers", which was the welcoming statement John and his comrades had received upon their arrival at the 'tin rest house'.

This speech was delivered by Colonel Nagitoma who was responsible for the administration of all the POW camps at the Burma end of the line. The Japanese had already had the trace of the line cut and camps built at five kilometre intervals along its length by Burmese, Malay and Tamil coolies. The terrain on this side of the border was infinitely preferable to that which lay between Bangkok and the Three Pagodas Pass on the Thailand side, where our men were forced to break the back of the most unyielding territory.

Nagitoma, in common with most of the Japanese captors, it seems, was not too fond of administration, or particularly good at it, so hence this duty was passed by him to the officers among their captives. It was at Thanbyuzayat that Brigadier Varley, Dudley's Australian counterpart, assumed overall control of all things pertaining to the men – camp movements, working parties, pay, 'hospitals' and, apparently, mountains of paperwork, which just goes to show that clerical duties are inescapable in any circumstances.

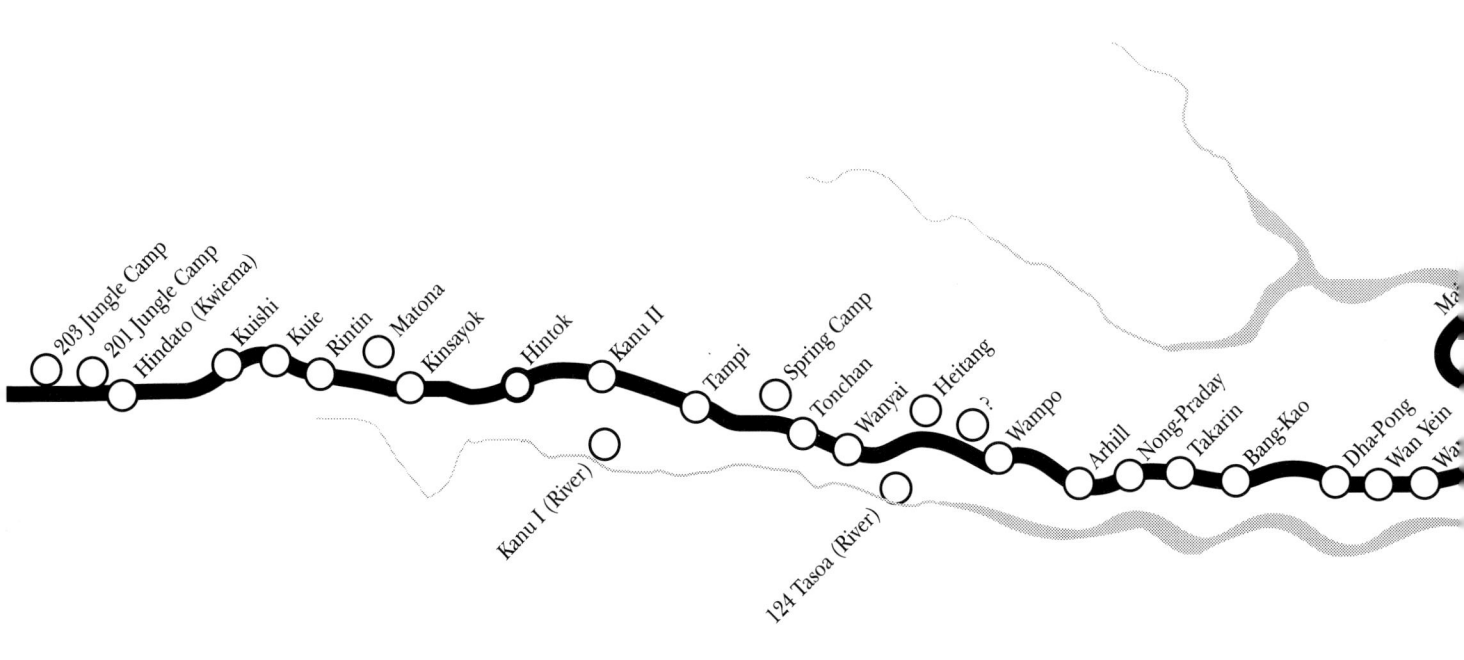

Great regret was felt by Dudley's Battalion that their leader was being superseded, but since the entire Burma Railway work force was united under single command in this way, they undoubtedly had greater bargaining power with the Japanese. Power which led to the formation of 'hospitals' and the seriously ill not being forced to work. The results of this were quite evident in the death rate in Burma compared to Thailand. What Brigadier Varley was unable to achieve was the necessary improvement in the supply of drugs and food. Nagitoma was not supplied with these and so the men never got them either. Many wasteful, criminal, futile losses of life were the result.

Dudley Apthorp, however, remained staunchly at the head of his own Battalion, who only stayed at Thanbyuzayat base camp for three days before moving on to the 18km camp, Helpauk. The sick remained at Thanbyuzayat, and the men would be sent back here as they became seriously ill until another hospital camp was established further up the line; the 55km camp, Khonkhan. 250 AMES lost another of their men at the base camp on the 29th of November 1942. LAC Frederick H Dobson "Dobbie", was 21 years of age.

Helpauk was known at the time and is remembered now as the 18km camp. All the camps in Burma were known by their distance from Thanbyuzayat, whereas in Thailand they were always referred to by name. The main reason for this is that although all the names were a

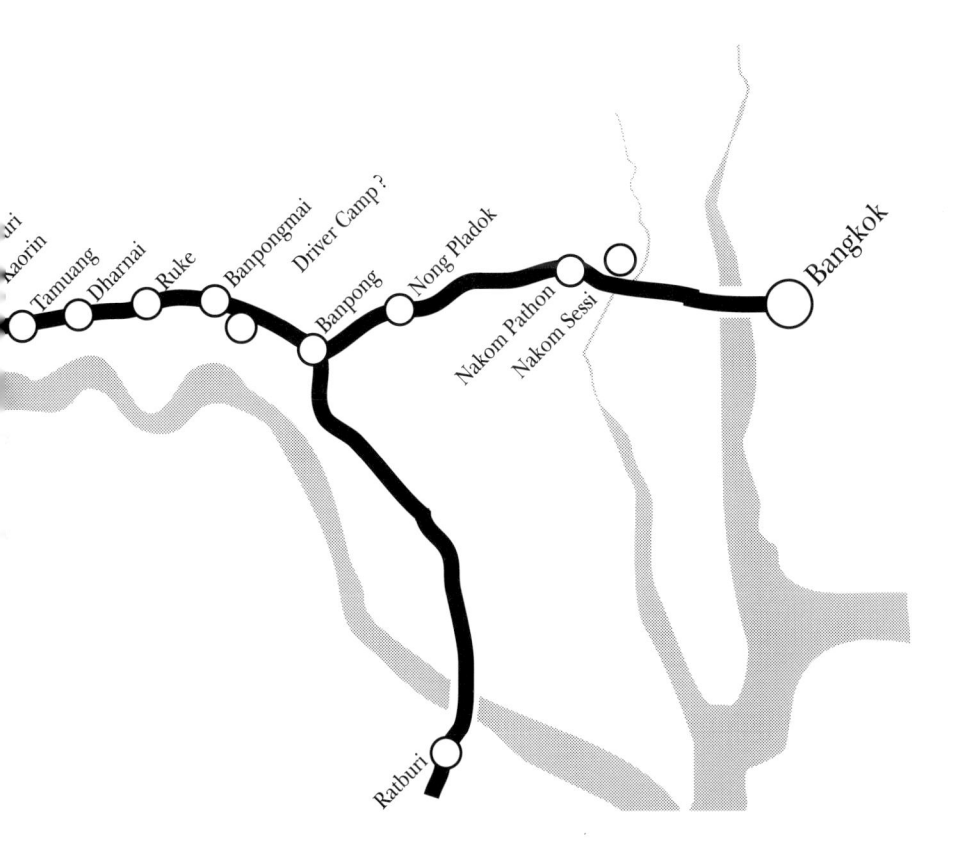

challenge to allied prisoners of war, they were often quite unpronounceable at the Burma end. All locations at both ends of the line have up to three spellings. The local name, the Japanese version, and then our mens' interpretation of the sound. Finding the correct one is sometimes difficult.

The Helpauk camp was in a valley, with an impressive range of hills on one side, and a more modest incline on the other. There were another 500 Australians in residence when the Battalion arrived and the camp was laid out typically with a square in the middle, the bamboo and palm huts for the men on two sides and the more salubrious quarters of the Japanese on one side. There was a cook house in the corner and a guard room at the gate, but the camps were never fenced, since there wasn't really anywhere to go. The jungle was its own prison.

All the camp's water came from a local stream and under Dudley's watchful eye the men established suitable washing and sanitary facilities within the first few days of their arrival. The Japanese had advanced the clock by two hours, presumably in line with Tokyo, and so roll-call was at eight, or six, depending on which way you looked at it, followed by a breakfast of rice porridge. This was basically achieved by boiling the rice too much, so that it became a sort of sludge. Sometimes there was a little salt to go with it. At Christmas, there was even a half-teaspoon of sugar.

Rice, Rice and More Bloody Rice

There is nothing wrong with rice. Rice is nice. It is the staple diet of the East and a highly nutritious food. Ironically, it is the classic bland food administered in the treatment of loose bowels. There were three basic problems with it on the Burma-Siam Railway. It was familiar to the men who were forced to eat it – or starve – as occasional rice pudding, served with sugar, lots of milk and perhaps some jam. It was not associated with main meals or as a savoury dish by men accustomed to meat with two vegetables and plenty of it.

The POW cooks did their best with it, but when it first arrived they had no idea how to cook such huge quantities of the stuff, and for quite a while it resembled badly mixed wallpaper paste. At Changi, where the men destined for the Thailand end of the line were held, it was literally inedible.

By far the biggest problem was that there was never enough of anything else to go with it. Sometimes there *was* nothing else to go with it. On the whole, a thin, watery stew went with it, composed of a few vegetables and strands of meat. This latter brew had to be constantly stirred up during serving so that everybody got a little bit of its precious contents.

After a while, quite good rice was at least coming out of the cook house, and they became terribly resourceful and clever with their basic product, making flour with it, which opened up other culinary possibilities. Corporal C Flanagan was in charge of the cook house for the British Sumatra Battalion and was recommended by Dudley for acknowledgement after the war. Whilst it has to be said that anyone working on the line would have swapped places with him at the drop of a hat, he worked hard to feed the men as well as he could on their return to camp.

The monotony and inadequacy of the diet went on and on. How many dreams there must have been of roast beef, shepherd's pie and sausages, but every morning saw the prospect of more rice. Colonel Coates used to say that their ticket home lay at the bottom of their mess tins. They ate their rice. They queued up for the scrapings around the sides of the cooking utensils. Burnt rice was a delicacy. They also loved a poem written by Captain W Store in Mergui, which became more pertinent during their years of captivity.

Unfortunately, four lines are omitted because they were considered too rude for publication in 1947, and I do not know them.

At the prison camp at Mergui,
Conditions were not nice
And we fed on a diet
That was wholly, solely rice.
Not rice as mother knew it,
Nor done as she used to do it – No!
Not baked rice nor flaked rice
With-sugar and with-milk rice,
Not cooked rice that looked rice
And all as smooth as silk – No!
We got glued rice, half stewed rice
Stone cold rice, grown old rice
Unfit for even dogs
The sort you throw to hogs.
We got broken rice, outspoken rice
That argued with your plate,
Unpolished rice, abolished rice
Some few years out of date.
We got burned rice, that wasn't rice
That tasted just like cinders
And brittle rice, sharp little rice
Like bits of festered tinders,

We got boiled rice, quite spoiled rice
And kerosene drum-oiled rice
That no one could call rice.
We got baked rice and caked rice
That weevils made their bed in.
We got bad rice, sad rice
That filled you with its sorrow.
We got podgy rice, stodgy rice
That meant no latrines tomorrow.
We got limed rice, grimed rice
And ought-to-have-been-crimed rice,
Disrupted rice, corrupted rice
Undischarged, bankrupted rice.
We got sloshed rice and squashed rice
But never any washed rice,
Half caste rice, half mast rice,
And lots of jungle-grassed rice.
We brewed rice, we chewed rice,
The lucky ones they spewed rice..
We starved on, but we lived on
In spite of everlasting rice.

Every ex-FEPOW I have the great pleasure to know still eats it.

There was a great prelude to the 'porridge' in the mornings. The bugle calls were supposed to be Japanese, but were delivered by a trumpeter, previously with a top American band. He jazzed them up so that they sounded different every time he played them, much to the annoyance of the Japanese.

At this early stage the men had a two hour lunch break at 12.30 and finished for the day at 6pm. Numerous fires would spring up all over the camp as they cooked whatever extras they could obtain. There was a camp canteen where eggs, bananas, sugar, coffee and tobacco could be bought, and the pay for a working man was ten cents a day.

Unfortunately, rapid and persistent inflation of the local currency rendered this sum more and more paltry, until ten days pay bought little more than one egg or two bananas, which wasn't a great help to dietary supplement.

To start with, 1.2 cubic metres of earth had to be dug up by each man and carried about a 100 yards to the embankment, but what the working parties did was to have men digging all day whilst other men would carry the earth in pairs in a basket suspended on a bamboo pole. On soft soil and with a relatively short distance to the embankment, in these quotas the work was tolerable. Would that it had stayed this way.

Rohan D Rivett, an Australian war correspondent who found himself upon the Burma-Siam Railway, sums it up so eloquently in his book 'Behind Bamboo':

> "Up and down the line, through untracked jungles, across dizzy ravines, astride rivers which became destructive torrents in the rains, through jungle-choked mountain passes, over rocky cliffs and through treacherous swamps, the toiling thousands of prisoners and conscripted Asiatics built this railway in conditions and under treatment which, if inflicted on animals at home, would produce an outcry from every decent man and woman in the community.

> It did not matter to the guards or the engineers who laid down the daily task how hard or difficult the ground, or what natural barriers obstructed the work. The fixed task had to be completed whether it meant seven hours of toil or ten or twelve. Day by day as, stretched over four hundred kilometres of jungle, the men from two score camps picked and dug, chunkeled and carried, the long hours and the fierce sun slowly drained away their resistance, never bolstered by a single square meal."

What he doesn't say, is that those 12 hours were stretched to 24 or even 36 before the Japanese had quite finished.

Two weeks after arrival at Helpauk, around the 9th of November 1942, the Japanese guards were replaced by Koreans. The Japanese treated the Koreans with the greatest contempt. On whom could they vent their anger and resentment? Torment, cruelty and humiliation were their specialities. One of their favourite games was to force their captives to punish each other, by lining up men facing one another and ordering them to slap each other's faces. A rifle or stick ensured that there were no half-hearted attempts made, but since the object of the exercise was to make the men lose their tempers, you can be sure that the Koreans never had the satisfaction of getting their own way.

Despite an absence of redeeming features, the Koreans did at least despise their bosses and would 'miscalculate' measurements on the line to get back to camp a little earlier, when it suited them.

Since humour crept in at times even in these most awful circumstances, it must be included to maintain the balance and since Spence Tracey of the Battalion has told a particular story so well in "The British Sumatra Battalion", I record it here in his own words:

> "It was at the 18 kilo that Pte Pagani, 28th Div Recce Corps, walked off. After seeing all the German escapes on TV, I think Pagani's was unique. I use the term 'walked off' because they were not camps as in Germany, with dogs, searchlights, etc., but just jungle. I remember the day quite well. There were three or four POWs talking to Pagani about his intentions.

> You'll never make it!" we told him. Then he said suddenly: "Well, so long, I'm off", and just walked away into the jungle.

> He had no gear, maybe that helped, also no waiting for it to get dark, or fences to climb, there was nothing to stop him. We wished him luck and that was it. It was Tenko when the Nips knew, he went about 2pm. We were all surprised that the Japs were not all that concerned. They told Dudley to send me to find him, by now it was 7pm. I was one of the 'lucky' ones to go under the command of 2nd Lt Villiers. The lads were all chockers to say the least. But Lt Villiers kept calling out, in the hope that Pagani was nearby, one of the best I thought was: "Come back Pagani, we know you don't mean it, you haven't got your water bottle!" I would think Pagani was the only POW to get away. Geographically he had a good start on anyone else and it was very sad he did not get home until 1945."

Their first Christmas was 'celebrated' in this camp and since the officers were persuaded by Dudley to chip in to a fund for the purpose, a reasonable dinner was produced for all. Steamed rice, sweet potatoes, boiled and fried peas, beans and fried bread (made with rice flour). Dessert was also made from rice flour and contained 52 eggs, but this considerable treat was divided between some 450 men.

The first 40 kilometres of the line were built in fairly flat terrain on the Burma side, including only one low range of hills at around the half-way mark. From here the Battalion moved on to the 35km camp, Tanyin, highly notable for an issue of clothes. A red rag to a bull to anyone unfortunate enough to have worked at the Thailand end of the line, to put this issue into perspective, welcome though it was it only gave one in ten men anything nearing completion and so divided between 450 it barely made any difference to their sorry situation.

100

Hunger was the biggest preoccupation, however, and Dudley's men proved extremely resourceful when it came to supplementing the meagre rations of whichever camp they found themselves in. Christened 'Appy's (Apthorp's) Locusts', they frequently stole food supplies from under the very noses of the Japanese, or traded with locals on peril of death.

At the 35km camp great friendship was forged with the Dutch. This was mainly brought about by dissension with a party of Americans who had arrived on the scene, and with whom the Battalion grudgingly joined forces.

Also at this camp one of the Japanese propaganda films was made to show the world how well they treated their prisoners. The only trouble was that all the delightful props they brought in for the purpose were promptly removed after filming. This included dummy drugs bottles which were completely empty anyway.

Next on the line was the 14km camp, Thetkaw, to which the Battalion moved on the 20th of March 1943. Rail laying was the job in hand. The rails weighed about 96 pounds per foot in length, and I would imagine it would have been about now that John dropped one of these rails on his foot. He lost his big toe nail, but he was very fortunate at the time, because the wound healed completely.

This was very skilled work, and in truth the men became rather adept at it; of necessity. They worked in teams and laid about two kilometres of track each day. Then the 'Speedo' period began, when the Japanese responsible for the building of the railway were under pressure to complete the line on schedule, the shifts grew longer and the men were pushed to work ever harder and faster. Night shifts worked by the light of improvised torches. The monsoons had begun. Fate had decreed that the rains would be worse this year than had been known before or afterwards.

No one had experienced hot water for over a year. The amount of meat they were receiving per man each day was roughly the equivalent in size to an Oxo cube. Their weight was seriously depleted; perhaps the average man down to six or seven stone, and although their lack of clothing may have been suited to the general daytime climate, building a railway is no joke without shoes, being permanently wet is not pleasant and cold nights without bedding is not funny at all.

They slept on bamboo ('the slats', they called them); a few had hammocks. If you were lucky you had a rice sack to cover you and keep you warm; even if you were sick. Even if you were dying. You lay with the bamboo digging into your bony back and if you had dysentery then you lay in that as well.

The 30km camp, Retpu, from the 14th of May, was notable for an issue of cards to send home. Every man was issued with one of these cards which had pre-printed messages on them for deletion as applicable, i.e. 'I am well/not well', 'I am working for pay', etc. At the bottom of the card there was a space for a personal message, but on the correct assumption that these cards would be censored, and since no one wanted to blow their only chance to let their loved ones know they were still alive, these were utilised with great caution by the men.

IMPERIAL JAPANESE ARMY

Date 19 · 5 · 1944

~~Your mails (and~~) ~~are received with thanks.~~
My health is (good, ~~usual, poor~~).
~~I am ill in hospital.~~
I am working for pay (~~I am paid monthly salary~~).
~~I am not working.~~
My best regards to *Miss M. Davidson + All Gilesgate Moor, Durham.*

Yours ever,

R. J. Bush

These cards were issued by the Japanese at Retpu for their prisoners to fill in and send home. Bob Bush was, not surprisingly, wishing his life away. He meant 1943.

Some put in cryptic messages thinking the artificiality of a 'tick card' may be too subtle for the folks back home. 'Tell Joe – he is a marine', was only one example, to indicate the untruth of the official message.

John filled in one of these cards and it did arrive home to Norbury Avenue in the course of time. He was well, he was working for pay, he signed it 'love, John' and he left it at that. He knew how the Davey's would react to this card just as it was, in his hand. He would not have hurt his mother by adding anything to what the Japanese were already spelling out to her.

IMPERIAL JAPANESE ARMY.

I am still in a P. O. W. Camp near Moulmein, Burma. There are 20,000 Prisoners, being Australian, Dutch, English, and American. There are several camps of 2/3000 prisoners who work at settled labour daily.

We are quartered in very plain huts. The climate is good. Our life is now easier with regard to food, medicine and clothes. The Japanese Commander sincerely endeavours to treat prisoners kindly.

Officers' salary is based on salary of Japanese Officers of the same rank and every prisoner who performs labour or duty is given daily wages from 25 cents (minimum) to 45 cents, according to rank and work.

Canteens are established where we can buy some extra foods and smokes. By courtesy of the Japanese Commander we conduct concerts in the camps, and a limited number go to a picture show about once per month.

Give My Love To Mary Hope You Are All Well. Am Looking Forward To Seeing You All Soon. Cheerio. All My Love, Bob.

Two cards from Bob Bush which arrived home during his captivity

IMPERIAL JAPANESE ARMY.

Our present place, quarters, and work is unchanged since last card sent to you The rains have finished, it is now beautiful weather. I am working healthily ( ). We receive newspapers printed in English which reveal world events.

We have joyfully received a present of some milk, tea, margarine, sugar and cigarettes from the Japanese Authorities.

We are very anxious to hear from home, but some prisoners have received letters or cables.

Everyone is hopeful of a speedy end to the war and with faith in the future we look forward to a happy reunion soon.

With best wishes for a cheerful Christmas.

Hoping You Are All Well. Give All My Love Mary Feel Sure Will Be Seeing You Soon

From   *R. J. Bush*

Another memorable incident at this camp was the Emperor's birthday, which was celebrated with a day off and Wagner and Schubert delivered by a full symphony orchestra in the jungle, which must have seemed quite unreal to everybody.

A lot of bowing and scraping went on in this camp whenever the Battalion were caught off their guard, since their captors seem to have been suffering from chips on the shoulder and this particular camp was 'graced' with a Japanese alcoholic officer who was obviously a complete nutcase. According to the Battalion members, when he left the camp in an armchair on the back of a truck and everyone had to line up to see him off, even the guards seem relieved to see him go. He was obviously 'removed' by his superiors because the camp was on the edge of collapse as a result of his lunacy.

Still the Battalion kept some semblance of humour in their lives. They had nicknames for all the guards. These included 'Donald Duck', 'Gold Tooth', 'Liver Lips', 'Cats Eyes', 'Mickey Rooney', 'Silver Bullet', 'Dillinger', 'BB' (Boy Bastard) and 'BBC' (Boy Bastard's Cobber).

The guards would beat the men with bamboo sticks. They shot some men to death and decapitated others. They would occasionally strap men's legs around poles with their knees bent and leave them there for hours, so that movement afterwards was barely possible.

Bob received this welcome reply from his fiancée – eventually.

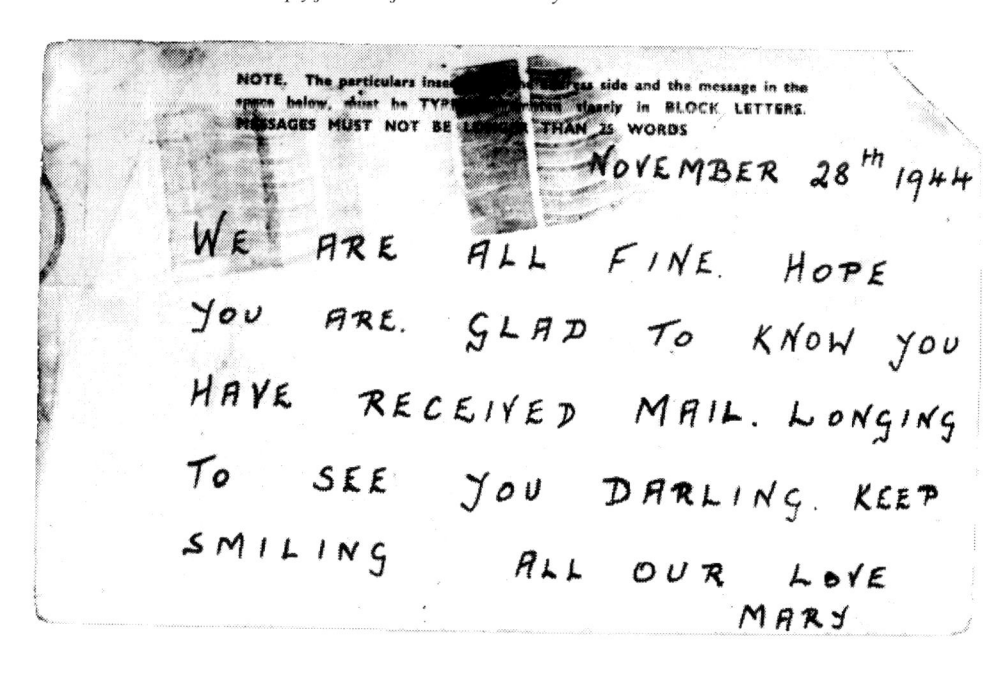

Despite their inadequate height compared to virtually all of their prisoners, they would punch them, if necessary standing on boxes to elevate them. Sometimes they would place the box on their victim's feet, as 6ft 6ins Peter Dunstan will testify.

On May the 15th four Liberator aircraft flew low over Thanbyuzayat, which had been bombed earlier in the year with considerable loss of POW life. This time, they turned west for a raid on Tavoy.

It was as the men marched to the 60km camp, Taungzun, that someone began to whistle 'Colonel Bogey'. Gradually, everyone followed suit. This is extraordinary, because somewhere in Thailand exactly the same thing had happened independently, and this defiant morale booster gave all of the men a rise in their spirits. This very English tune is synonymous with everything which was the Burma-Siam Railway.

It was good that the men whistled, because the fine Australian band which had once accompanied them had been eroded by deaths, reaction of instruments to humidity and doubtless a few trade-offs in local markets.

"I had to kill one hundred flies before I claimed my evening meal."
Charles Peall. 18th July 1994

Large numbers of any living species in close proximity create a breeding ground for disease. Combine this with unsanitary conditions – such as open latrines in which millions of flies perpetuated their own kind, overflowing in the relentless monsoons of 1943 – and severe illness becomes a foregone conclusion.

Diarrhoea, together with blood and mucus, is a symptom of many underlying disorders from gastroenteritis (due to bacterial enterotoxins), haemorrhagic colitis, shigellosis (bacillary dysentery) to amoebiasis (amoebic dysentery). All are accompanied by abdominal cramps and fever. All of the men suffered from it in one form or another.

These conditions are all treatable, but equally, can all be dangerous, especially in debilitated patients and at the onset of complications. The main side-effect is dehydration.

The causes are commonly contaminated food, polluted water, poor sanitation and flies. Entry of the bacteria to the body is via the mouth.

Strict hygiene – proper isolation of faeces and patients, thorough hand washing, the storage of soiled linen in covered buckets of soap and water prior to boiling, are obvious pre-requisites to treatment. Appropriate drugs should be administered (*not* antibiotics) and supportive care with fluids and a bland diet.

In the case of amoebiasis, which in itself covers mild diarrhoea to dysentery, it is common in the tropics and thrives in warm, moist, unsanitary conditions. Amoebic dysentery which is the most severe form, at its worst, produces anaemia and emaciation. It can lead to liver infection, which in turn spreads to the lungs.

A chemist could administer the treatment and there are many options, even standbys, to allow for availability, but the most commonly recommended are metronidazole and emetine. As a total medical layman, I would say if you had either of these you were more than halfway there.

The 55km camp, Khonkhan, in which John died from what I understand to be amoebic dysentery – a 'hospital camp', as described by the Japanese – had condy's crystals and ground charcoal. That was it. They also had no soap. Disinfectant on this scenic railway was the stuff which dreams are made of.

John also had malaria.

The medical orderlies reported to the Japanese that they were suffering many fatalities from what they believed to be amoebic dysentery. They asked for emetine. The refusal from the Japanese was accompanied by the assurance that the men were suffering 'hill diarrhoea' and that the word 'dysentery' was not to be used on death certificates, which they later destroyed anyway.

Somehow, the 55km camp acquired a microscope. They were able to provide their captors with concrete proof of the presence of amoebic parasites. Still, they never got their emetine.

Cholera was probably the most dreaded disease which lurked on the railway. This was usually a one-way ticket, and the Japanese feared catching it so much they actually inoculated quite a few POWs against it. It still did its work.

Even cholera could be either a mild, uncomplicated episode of diarrhoea, or a deadly disease. Abrupt, painless, watery diarrhoea and vomiting are usually the initial symptoms. Severe water depletion leads to intense thirst, the excretion of an abnormally small amount of urine, muscle cramps, weakness and marked degeneration of tissue, with sunken eyes and wrinkling of skin on the fingers.

In severe cases which are untreated, the fatality rate can be 50%. This drops to 1% with prompt and adequate fluid therapy and relevant treatment. Proper disposal of human excrement and purification of water supplies are essential to the control of the disease.

With dead bodies floating in their water sources, sanitation was an almost uncontrollable problem, and it got worse. 'Romusha', forced labour, namely 'Asian persons who were forced

106

to work heavily during Japanese occupation', from Thailand, Burma, Malaysia, Indonesia and Vietnam, tended not to bury their dead. It is estimated that out of approximately 200,000 of them, between 80,000 – 100,000 perished. It is further believed that the total number of Romusha was closer to 270,000, of which only 35,000 were repatriated after the war.

These poor souls were lured by the Japanese to their fate on the promise of employment and good wages. Sometimes they were just press-ganged. They had no command, no order, no discipline and little notion of hygiene. They died in their thousands and their rotting corpses added further fuel to the general putrefaction.

A diet which consisted largely of only rice, supplemented by a thin, watery stew, caused malnutrition and general vitamin deficiency on a grand scale. This exacerbated illness from disease, and hampered or prevented recovery, but it also caused widespread disorders, all by itself.

Thiamine (vitamin B1) deficiency, beriberi, arose from inadequate intake, (particularly prevalent in people subsisting on highly polished rice) and impaired absorption of nutrients caused by long-continued diarrhoeas. You don't have to be a medical expert to understand how one thing led to another.

Early deficiency produces fatigue, irritation, poor memory, sleep disturbances, anorexia, abdominal discomfort and constipation, burning of the feet, (particularly severe at night), calf muscle cramps, pains in the legs, atrophy of the calf and thigh muscles. The arms may become involved after leg signs are well established. It is ironic that the medical books do not describe what this condition leads to if it is neglected of necessity, i.e the prescribed treatment, vitamin B1,(would you believe?), is not available. In short this was a grotesque swelling of the body, as if the flesh and muscle were dropping to the lowest point of gravity in a great heap. Tissue became spongy to the touch. This was dry beriberi. The wet version literally drowned you from the inside.

Pellagra – niacin (nicotinic acid) deficiency is in some ways a similar disorder when it remains untreated. It makes itself apparent in inflammation of the mouth and tongue, diarrhoea, dermatitis, delirium or dementia. Dry, scaly, inelastic skin too large for the part it covers is further aggravated by sunlight. The elementary treatment is niacinamide and a good, balanced diet. No chance. Many men have described this condition causing burning feet, on which they could not stand still, nor forget in order to catch some sleep when it was so badly needed.

There were numerous disorders which dogged these long suffering men, caused by humidity or malnutrition, and certainly inordinately grim when the two worked in cahoots and there was no respite. 'Changi balls', or 'rice balls' speak for themselves. There wasn't a man to be found without a weeping rash or skin disorder of some description.

A good, well balanced diet, heavy on nutrients – if bland in consistency – are essential to the recovery of any patient. Administered with care in co-ordination with drugs and medicines, they complement one another and maximise the chances of recovery.

Sick men didn't work. Sick men were not expending energy, therefore they didn't need so much nourishment, did they? Half rations, at best, were the order of the day. The Japanese had a particularly inhumane approach to the 55km camp in Burma. They would weigh the inmates, suffering in the main from dysentery, beriberi and tropical ulcers. As their body weight diminished from lack of food and from their wasting illnesses, the food rations were further reduced accordingly.

There were other life threatening disorders, rife in the tropics, from which again virtually everybody suffered. There was simply no escape from their prevalence.

The infection of malaria occurs through the bite of an infected female anopheles mosquito. Malarial parasites of four species affect man. They multiply within the liver cells and from there, enter into the bloodstream.

Certainly potentially lethal if unchecked, malaria manifests itself in fever, malaise, headache and chills. It varies in its voracity between victims, and depending on the prevailing circumstances. Blackwater fever is a rare complication and can occur in sufferers of chronic malaria who are treated with quinine.

Otherwise, quinine or quinidine is the principal treatment and because of its reduced efficacy in Thailand and other parts of South East Asia, this should be administered for seven days.

Some quinine was available along the line, but in pathetically small quantities. It would be given to those who appeared to need it most, but the chronic cases were, according to medical opinion, not the most appropriate recipients. I know of one such receiver of this treatment who subsequently suffered the repercussions and still survived – Bob Bush. Testimony to the rarity of quinine, at the time, he did not receive very much. Had greater quantities of quinine been available it would, however, have brought welcome relief to a great many sufferers and would have prevented deaths.

As if these vile disorders were not enough to contend with, Nature had something else up her sleeve. Something so dreadful to throw into this already festering melting pot, it does not bear thinking about. Tropical ulcers, which might start as insignificantly as a pimple, could strip a man's leg to the bone with horrifying speed in the grossly unfortunate.

Apart from dangling ones legs in the river to allow the fish to eat at the infection (which gave the men great satisfaction when the fish were caught and eaten by their guards), the only treatment available for this grotesque condition was condy's crystals, the deliberate introduction of maggots to the infected area, or, more commonly, the gouging out of the poisoned flesh with the aid of a sharpened spoon. The screams, and the smell from the huts of the afflicted, will remain with those who witnessed them for all time.

In really serious cases, amputation was the only way to prevent death. Anaesthetics were, mercifully, available – some of the time. Post-operative trauma was, however, a recorded cause of death in many instances, since surgery of only the crudest order was all that even brilliant surgeons had the facilities to perform.

There probably isn't an ex-FEPOW alive who does not have scars from such ulcers which, thankfully, in most men did not get out of hand.

I don't know how they were caused, but I would imagine that the climate and the unhealthy conditions had more than a little to do with men developing these ulcers; commonly from every scratch and injury sustained in the building of the railway, in bare feet and 'Jap happys', which were basically loincloths constructed out of remaining uniform fragments.

There were of course far more injuries sustained in this way. Broken limbs, abrasions and even fatalities from falling were not uncommon, especially in the central territory, where the two ends of the line met in the mountainous land which separates Burma from Thailand. It was also in this fearful place that supplies were at their very minimum, through transportation difficulties, or lack of effort, depending on how you look at it.

Here, the terrain was the hardest to break and the conditions were at their worst. As the work progressed, and both sides became nearer to this most gruesome 'Checkpoint Charlie', completion was behind schedule and the Japanese applied further pressure to speed things along. The monsoons raged.

And into this cauldron of disaster went other ingredients besides. I hesitate to use the word overwork, because this does not adequately describe the shifts which sent men to the line in the dark of morning and back to camp in the dark of night.

Overwork combined with underfeeding has inevitable consequences, weakening defences and increasing vulnerability to disease. In some camps, conditions were worse than in others, so that the general state of the men would often deteriorate from low to lower, and in many cases, beyond.

John was lucky. Dudley Apthorp protected his sick from further work. Many others were not so fortunate. There was not a single man on the line who would not have been hospitalised by a civilised culture.

The relationship between the nature of the illnesses, some caused by poor diet and others exacerbated by malnutrition, and the prevailing unhealthy conditions and poor sanitation, are intrinsically linked. Prevention was impossible to control. Malaria was widespread and diarrhoea a virtually permanent condition. It was simply a question of luck in the end, whether more serious disorders were contracted; by whom, and how severe they became.

Without any improvements in hygiene, sanitation or general underlying conditions being made possible, with even the simple provision of soap or disinfectant, the risk of further infection was compounded.

The withholding of drugs and medicines with which to treat the sick effectively guaranteed fatalities and further outbreaks.

The Burma-Siam Railway was a death sentence.

Is there a single example in the whole of the history of the world of the fates conspiring quite so completely to endanger life, without any respite or compassion of any description? I think not.

Further and further north and to their peril, went the men at the Thailand end of the line. Further and further south went the men at the Burma end. Until what was left of them met in the middle.

A golden spike was laid into the railway by the Japanese in celebration of the completion of their impossible feat of engineering. A feat which they had said in every camp, to every man, would be fulfilled over their dead bodies – if necessary using them as sleepers. Their prophecy was fulfilled. Their bloody railway was in position, and all along it lay the corpses of the men whose lives it had cost to build.

"When the man on the lake says come in number six – your time is up."

Arthur Hargest, 15th June 1994

The Battalion had already been forewarned of the delights which awaited them at Taungzun, where the two kilometre walk to work and back occupied the men's camp time. A timber bridge en route began to collapse under the combined pressures of a fallen road bridge and all its resultant debris, together with logs, branches and mud delivered with the severe monsoons which raged in this dreadful year.

The rebuilding of the bridge entailed extra work for the men and the enormous number of tree trunks they had to cut and place created traps for unwary legs. The endless rain was cold at night but the men toiled on in their loincloths just the same, assisted by elephants and plagued by insects, the worst of which were fruit beetles the size of golf balls.

As the rains continued ceaselessly, the new bridge collapsed just as the old one had done, built, as it was, under Japanese command along the same lines as its predecessor. Not only did John and the rest of the battalion have to endure this back-breaking futility, their camp was reduced to a sea of liquid mud with the latrine overflow yielding millions of maggots and blue bottle flies. The food was as inadequate as ever.

Dudley Apthorp understood very well that the survival of his men depended as much as anything upon their mental fortitude. They would call upon the padre, or Dudley, to recite the Lord's Prayer, or the 23rd Psalm, from which they derived great comfort and strength, and it had to be the *traditional* version. Dudley was most emphatic (and absolutely right) about this.

> *The Lord is my shepherd; I shall not want.*
> *He maketh me to lie down in green pastures; He leadeth me beside the still waters.*
> *He restoreth my soul; He leadeth me in the paths of righteousness for his name's sake.*
> *Yea, though I walk through the valley of the shadow of death, I will fear no evil; for thou art with me;*
>   *thy rod and thy staff they comfort me.*
> *Thou preparest a table before me in the presence of mine enemies; Thou annointest my head with oil;*
>   *my cup runneth over.*
> *Surely goodness and mercy shall follow me all the days of my life; and I will dwell in the house of the*
>   *Lord forever.*

By the 14th of November 1943 the Battalion had moved to the very worst camp they were to encounter, the 114km camp, Chaungena. They were transported in two parties over the course of nearly one month.

Only the sick were left behind. John Davey became separated at the 60km camp from the Sumatra Battalion for the first time, and from what was left of his original unit, 250 AMES, for the last time. Before Arthur Hargest left for Chaungena, he went to visit his friend. He found John in good spirits. Smiling, clean shaven and sketching in an exercise book, John was not unduly underweight. He looked quite good – like himself, and he certainly was his good humoured self that day. Arthur was concerned, however, to find John sitting up on a stretcher bed, normally associated with patients who could not fend for themselves. He discreetly enquired of the MO as he left whether John was in danger. The reply he received was "not yet". Arthur didn't much like the sound of this. Not long after the Battalion's departure, John was moved back to the 55km camp, Khonkhan.

The 55km camp had its own padre and MO's who could not have been more dedicated to their duties. It was also graced by the presence of Colonel Sir Albert Coates, AIF, by whom any private patient would have been honoured to have been overseen. What they totally lacked in drugs and even basic medical facilities, they tried to make up for as best they could with improvisation, imagination and care and I don't think that in the circumstances John could possibly have been in better hands.

Because Khonkhan was a 'hospital' camp, and housed no working men, the food rations were appalling. When the camp appealed to the Japanese to be allowed to supplement their pathetic rations by obtaining their own locally available supplies, permission was refused.

The grounds on which this refusal was made was as follows: 'Under the Geneva Convention, you should get these things from us. If you have to buy them, it means we are not giving you enough. If we stop you from buying these things, therefore, it means you are getting enough'. So that was that, except trading did go on with the Burmese and skinny cattle were brought into camp under cover of darkness. Also, Raymond Frazer, a Battalion member and friend to John was resident in this camp, and he risked his life with a trading racket which doubtless saved many others.

Somehow, John had kept his watch. He wasn't allowed to have this, so he must have hidden it very well throughout his captivity to be able to produce it now, when he needed it the most, or rather, what it could buy. Raymond Frazer sold John's watch for him and with the money John was able to acquire fish, vegetables and eggs. Had he had these precious commodities earlier he might have been saved. Dysentery is a very debilitating disease which drains nutrients at an alarming rate. Even though you would not wish to eat with stomach cramps and fever, all the men were painfully aware that without food, whatever was available and no matter how inadequate, then death was inevitable. Death by emaciation.

It is because of John's canniness in keeping his watch and his acquisition of vitamins, no matter how late they came, that I know my uncle had absolutely no intention of dying in this dreadful place. He had kept his head down and knuckled under with his captivity. Despite the inevitable cynicism which had crept into the general mentality of John and his mates, they had maintained their strength, sanity, good humour and bloody mindedness about getting on with it, getting liberated and getting the hell out and going home.

Meanwhile, at the 114km camp, things were as bad as they were ever going to get. At the very border of Thailand near to the Three Pagodas Pass, Chaungena camp had been built on a steep incline. Apart from the food being the worst the men had ever encountered, the overwork in the worst monsoons the country was to encounter in recorded history having taken its inevitable toll on the men and the odd orang-utan sharing the latrines, there was nothing to set this camp aside from any other which had already been experienced to the full. Other than pellagra and beriberi on top of everything else.

Only some 300 men remained of the 480 who had started out from Padang in Sumatra in May 1942. At least 86 of them were in graves along the line. About 50 of the men were at the 55km 'hospital' camp. Some were at the base camp at Thanbyuzayat.

It was at Chaungena that the expression "attap staring" was coined. It referred to a condition whereby the victim would lose the will to go on, withdraw totally from his comrades, and endlessly stare at the bamboo walls or roof of his hut. Some of these men died.

Khonkhan's patients consisted mostly of dysentery cases and serious tropical ulcers, which necessitated 110 amputations. Of Colonel Coates amputees in this camp only 40 survived; their deaths being from gangrene and/or dysentery. John would have been 'treated' with ground charcoal. There was nothing else available.

The dysentery hut was known as the 'death house' both in Burma and in Thailand. At Khonkhan this was a gloomy hut with a 'thunder box', as the Australians called it, in the centre aisle. For the many patients who could not make it to the centre aisle, there were no bedpans, so tin cans, old mess tins, half coconut shells or bamboo pots were utilised instead. There was, of course, no toilet paper on the Burma-Siam Railway.

I don't know how John spent the last weeks of his life, other than this. I believe that he would have fought his illness like the devil and I also know that he would have shown the same consideration to others that he had maintained until his illness struck, which all his comrades have vouched for.

Fellow Battalion members came and went; some of them even went back on the line, which was not a great incentive for recovery. Even a fellow 250 AMES pal, Bob Bush, was sent to the 55km camp where he was placed next to John. Bob was in a very bad way with dysentery and was not expected to survive, either by Dudley or his comrades.

John was an extremely sick man, but since Bob was also clearly very ill indeed, he does not remember having any conversation with John, nor anything about John's state, other than that he was no more emaciated than the rest of them.

The main thing, however, is that Bob knew that he was next to John. I'm quite sure that John also knew that he was next to Bob. John would have kept his eggs in what passed for a pillow, which would have been a bit of rice sack. The standard tactic, if you were lucky enough to have eggs (probably duck), was to eke them out and eat one a day, if you could.

In Thailand, where the very sick were generally still with their mates, despite horrendous deaths in proportion to their numbers, much 'force feeding' saved a lot of lives. If a sick man vomited his rice, his mates would pick up grain by grain and shove them back in his mouth.

The orderlies at the Burma 'hospital' camps were as dedicated a bunch of men as you would ever find, anywhere. British and Australians toiled day and night to save lives with no facilities to assist them. Whoever John encountered at any time in his final weeks would have been decent and kind to him, just as they were to everybody.

During the early, dark hours of the 27th of December 1943, John Edwin Davey drifted into sleep and into death. He attained his liberation earlier than many, but for his freedom, he paid a terrible price.

He never intended to die. Physical weakness and debility got the better of him in the end, but his will power never faltered. John wanted to live every bit as much as we all wish that he had lived. He was an exceptional man. We will always love him.

"And Jesus said unto them, I am the bread of life: he that cometh to me shall never hunger: and he that believeth in me shall never thirst." St John VI

"....(John) died very quietly, just as he always lived." Raymond Frazer.

British Sumatra Battalion chronological casualties by date at the 55km camp, Khonkhan:

Gnr Bradley, R W	19.9.43	Gnr Bachl, W C	15.11.43
Ck Simcock, HC	1.10.43	Gnr Hutchinson, N	15.11.43
Gnr Bicknell, S	3.10.43	Gnr Smith, W	17.11.43
Pte Bailey, N C	4.10.43	L/S Hopkins, R H	22.11.43
A/B McLachlan, E J R	10.11.43	Pte Arnold, H	25.11.43
Pte Bland, J	13.11.43	Gnr Yarwood, S A R	3.12.43
Cpl Bostock, D	13.11.43	Gnr Thomson, T H	14.12.43
Pte Swalwell, J	13.11.43	O/S Foster, S A	22.12.43
Gnr Gough, F W	14.11.43	L/Bdr Laird, G	22.12.43
Gnr Russell, F	14.11.43	Cpl Davey, J E	27.12.43

Aftermath

News of John's death travelled to the 114km camp and the remainder of the Battalion as quickly as if they'd had a fax machine. There was shock at the news, despite the MO's prognosis, given to Arthur. There was genuine regard felt by John's mates, even though they'd buried ten men at their working camp in the preceding two days alone. Another 29 were to die here before the Battalion left on the 12th of January 1944.

The same news was not to reach home and John's family for almost another two years. The fact that John was still 'missing' after other prisoners of war of the Japanese had safely returned killed John's mother in the interim. The details of his death, as precisely as they can probably ever be known, were not to be revealed to us for over 50 years.

Bob Bush awoke on the 27th of December to find himself lying between two dead men. One of them was my uncle John, the other poor soul was unknown to him. I can only try to imagine the feelings of this kind man, who was so very sick. I'm quite sure it would have shocked him dreadfully, and I hope that perhaps this saved his own life.

I wish I could have held John's hand when he died.

The 55km camp, Khonkhan was closed down at the end of December 1943, and the surviving POWs were sent to Tamarkan in Thailand. Approximately 430 bodies remained in the nearby cemetery. 'Shrouded' in one or two rice sacks, my uncle John was one of them.

Our lost men from the Burma end of the line who could be found and properly identified from records were placed in wood coffins and re-buried in Thanbyuzayat War Cemetery after the war. Of the 3,771 graves there, almost 3,000 resulted from deaths in the monsoons and 'speedos' of 1943.

Disease was still rife at the 114km working camp, and men were suffering from dysentery, malaria and tropical ulcers as well as beriberi and pellegra. A Dutch doctor at Chaungena, Dr. Hekan, showed the men which plants nearby were of the most value, nutritionally as well as for medicinal purposes. In return they taught him English; much of it consisting of four-letter words.

Had Arthur Hargest, Jim Hall, Joe White and the others not got out of the 114km camp when they did then there would be very few left today to tell the tale. Bob Bush also got out of the 55km camp and although he went on to suffer blackwater fever, he still survived. Even the

Japanese conceded Chaungena so bad that it was evacuated, and although some men were left behind for maintenance, the remainder of the sad remnants of the camp's occupants went on to Kanchanaburi.

It was here that their journey was carried out on the railway which the men had built and although there was some sweet justice in the fruits of their labours carrying them to ultimate safety, many fingers must have been crossed that the sabotage in its construction at both ends of the line would not make itself apparent just yet.

The train passed through mountainous country and at times along a sheer cliff face. The men saw one range of hills after another, and only then did they realise how much worse the terrain had been for the men on the other side of the line. They were thankful that they had toiled in Burma, and those are their words and not mine.

It was at Kanchanaburi that the British from the Burma end of the line met with other British from the Thailand end, for the first time. Much information was exchanged, and doubtless many new friendships forged as well. Dudley's lot had rubbed shoulders with Australians, Dutch and Americans, but you can't beat your own kind, and in these circumstances it must have seemed like somebody's birthday.

Part of the officers' pay, which had always been superior to other ranks, was by this time being contributed to a central fund in order to buy food for the sick. The death rate decreased dramatically. Railway work was completed, medical facilities improved, general conditions were better. Jolly good show. The dead were dead and will forever remain dead. All in their prime or a good number of years away from it. Those who lie in jungle graves will never, ever come home. Why did *they* have to die?

Epilogue

John's short story ends with his death on the 27th of December 1943, but the story of his friends went on to liberation. Perhaps they will all realise my love for them that I carry on to finish their dreadful tale when I left my heart in Khonkhan.

Even at Kanchanaburi, many sick were left behind by the British Sumatra Battalion. A party of Kumies, as the Japanese called them, had to be found to go to Japan. The Japanese sincerely harboured fantasies of having allied slaves to enrich the remainder of their honourable lives at this time. Parties were to be made up of Australian, Dutch and American also.

Dudley managed to round up one 114 men for this dubious privilege, declared fit by a Japanese 'doctor', in view of their ability to hold their fingers in the air and wiggle them around. Bob Bush, who was in dire straits, was not among this party. Nor was Joe White nor Arthur Hargest. Only Jim Hall; but bar the final agonies, it was almost over for all of them. It was over for John, too, but in a different way. I still look at the casualty lists in the book written from Dudley Apthorp's records and think that if I could only eliminate his death from the book then I could bring him back to life.

51 Kumi, as Dudley's group was now known, was issued for the first and last time with footwear, underclothes, jackets and shorts. The men were searched for contraband, but still left for Kanchanaburi station carrying their knives, wire, tools and cherished possessions with which they were left.

After a six mile march the train took them to Nong Pla Duk and from here, via Bangkok, 400 miles to Phnom Penh on the Mekong River. The remainder of their journey to Saigon was by barge. Here, Dudley embraced another 13 men into the remains of his Battalion, who were British civilians enlisted in the Dutch army.

Even on this journey, things were only 'better' because things had been so unbelievably awful. Lack of water, let alone food, was a problem, and the 'British Sumatra Battalion' book describes an urgent issue of a light brown substance as 'tea', when heaven only knows what it really was. Dudley still had his in a much cherished china cup and saucer; kept mysteriously intact, as was the fact that he had obtained it in the first place.

Saigon was described to the prisoners as being a camp of well built barracks with running water and electric light, where food could be bought without stint in the well-stocked canteen.

This had all been heard before. The Japanese had told the prisoners of Changi that their unknown destination of the Burma-Siam Railway was a rest camp, in which the sick could recuperate. Some scepticism was felt by all in the anticipation of their new destination, but the relief in leaving behind the railway gave its own, considerable lift.

In fact, Saigon wasn't too bad at all, and the testimony to this is that only one death occurred in the Battalion in almost a year. The Vichy French were very friendly and supplied badly needed medicines. Water really was available and *clean*. Food was far more plentiful and the work, although hard on the docks and aerodrome, was nevertheless a huge improvement on the railway.

Three 40 watt bulbs provided the electric light in the huts, which were made of wood! (Not bamboo), although some bright spark had decreed that the 'hospital' huts should be constructed of bamboo with attap roofs, presumably to keep the sick in the manner to which they had become accustomed.

The Japanese hadn't changed in their treatment of their prisoners, but, the biggest boost to morale the men were experiencing was the news. The allies were winning!

———————

On February the 14th, 1945, the RAF and US Air Force reduced Dresden to a smoking ruin. On the 20th, Churchill and Roosevelt met in Cairo to discuss the war against Japan. By the 5th of March, the British had captured the Japanese base of Meiktila, cutting Burma in two.

Lloyd George passed away aged 82, with his daughter holding one hand and his wife the other, on the 26th.

Roosevelt died on April the 12th, on the very eve of victory. Hitler killed himself on the 30th. Belsen was discovered by British soldiers on the same day. Just one heap of rotting corpses of unclothed women, measured 80 yards in length, 30 yards in width and four feet in height.

On May the 3rd the British 14th Army took Rangoon and on the 17th the Royal Navy battled with the Japanese in the Malacca Straits.

As Big Ben chimed at 3pm on May the 8th, Churchill broadcast to the nation that although Japan remained to be subdued, the war in Europe would end at midnight. "Advance Britannia!", he proclaimed. "Long live the cause of freedom! God save the King!"

In June, the Japanese called for all POW officers of all nationalities to be assembled at Nakhon Nayok in Thailand. A new camp was to be set up for them and the officers slept in the open air until first tents were provided and then the familiar bamboo and attap huts.

118

On August the 6th and 9th respectively, US Army Air Corps' Super-Fortress aircraft, dropped atomic bombs on Hiroshima and Nagasaki.

Japan surrendered unconditionally on August the 14th, 1945. The war was over. So were more than 55 million casualties. One of them was my uncle John.

After the defeat of the Japanese the new officers' camp at Nakhon Nayok was found to be surrounded by trucks mounted with machine guns – all pointing inwards. So was the mens' camp in Saigon.

One night in September, all the guards disappeared. The officers were informed by an American paratrooper the next day that the Japanese had been defeated.

Needless to say, nobody told the men in Saigon. They only knew that something was up because planes were dropping articles of clothing and the French were being nice to them.

For some Thailand POWs, after three and a half years of near starvation, their first air-drop was of condoms. About 10,000 of them – with no flavour.

The Death Railway at Chong Kai, Thailand.

The French *were* very kind, and perceptive. They felt that the men they helped and cared for were so grateful for every little kindness and to become part of family life, even though it was someone else's family. The French recognised a parallel between the mens' noble demeanour and Kipling's famous poem line..."If you can wait and not be tired of waiting."

An article published in 'Le Temps de Saigon' on the 24th of December, 1945, headed 'Reminiscences on our friends the British POWs', included the following:

> *"Only occasionally, a sudden poignant expression – a handshake a little too hard, lasting too long – or suddenly a voice a little hoarse; their spirit, their morale, seemed untouched. Had they really passed through the hell of that abominable construction – the Burma-Siam Railway – these men, unsoured, perfectly sane and perfectly healthy in judgement. Had they truly been humiliated, maltreated, tortured day after day for years; these men, obviously educated, whose whole behaviour in our homes is perfectly gentlemanly."*

Work, spirit and humour were the only Allied weapons on the Burma-Siam Railway, and the French saw in our men just what had brought them through and kept them intact. Faith.

Thank God these men came home. So many others never will.

The cost of World War Two

British & Commonwealth	*over*	500,000
France	*over*	600,000
United States	*over*	300,000
USSR	*over*	21,300,000
Poland	*over*	7,400,000
Yugoslavia	*over*	1,600,000
China	*over*	13,500,000
Germany	*over*	7,000,000
Austria	*over*	300,000
Japan	*over*	2,000,000
		deaths

Of over 55 million casualties in total, *over* 30 million were civilians. The figures above tell only a part of the story. They do not include losses for the whole of Europe. They cannot include losses for the whole of the Commonwealth. For example, they would not take account of the unknown total of Burmese and Malaysian civilians who lost their lives on the Burma-Siam Railway.

Not to reproduce these figures because they are vague and omit some of our allies – particularly the Dutch – in view of the subject matter of this book, would be a wasted opportunity. To present them illustrates the enormity of the consequences of global warfare upon human beings.

Part III **The Pilgrimage**

Of the fact that it required lies and deceit to obtain a visa to travel to Myanmar I am not in the least ashamed. This was simply the only way in which I would acquire a visa and so I dutifully obliged the authorities with the information they wanted to hear. Yes, I was travelling through Burma under the constant guidance of a specialist tour company (true enough) and I carried a letter from them confirming that I would be travelling from Rangoon to Mandalay and on to other delightful, recognised tourist resorts further north. (Lies, lies and more lies).

I was going to Rangoon alright, but from there I was travelling strictly off-limits south into Martaban and on to even more off-limits Moulmein and beyond to 'out of the question off-limits' Thanbyuzayat and my final goal. As I sat in the Myanmar Embassy in London awaiting the return of my passport, every time somebody moved I flinched and when an official came and sat beside me, I must surely have looked more like Burma's ultimate political enemy than a humble pilgrim.

When the official handed me my passport complete with visa it took all of my willpower to remain engaged in polite conversation about having a nice time in Mandalay. I wanted to grab my papers and run like hell. All pleasantries exchanged I quietly got up and left, being sure to say goodbye to every single person as I went. I tried to do it slowly but still felt as if I was going too fast and drawing attention to my guilt. Once around the corner from the Embassy on a sunny London street I let go of my restraint and shouted, 'ya hoo'!

In under a month I would be in Burma at last. On the 22nd of November 1994 I would stand before John's grave, clutching the biggest wreath I could buy, which had been touched by all of John's family and containing a card signed by his 250 AMES mates. There was a lot to do to get ready physically for the trip with the inevitable shopping and packing of ultimately unsuitable things as well as essentials. I had hepatitis boosts, rabies injections and bought at least a years' supply of anti-malarial devices and antidotes. To prepare mentally was too big a challenge in the time but the drive to get on and just do it was more than powerful enough to see me through.

Our journey of a lifetime would involve four flights, three train journeys and umpteen cars and mini-buses. It would span two countries, the other being Thailand, in which Peter Dunstan, through his personal experience of the Burma-Siam Railway at the Thailand end, proved an intrepid guide. It all started in Bangkok, in which we left whatever luggage was not required for the fulfilment of our mission in Burma and then at last we were on our way.

To fully appreciate the impact of the adventure when it was finally being experienced, you have to remember how long the build-up to it actually was. Even when it was successfully under way there were interminable delays whilst we travelled from a to b, stopping along the way to appreciate other ports of call, admiring temples and catching sleep, which at times had to be sacrificed to the cause. At every stage once in Burma it was quite likely that our journey would be halted by a refusal for us to continue. This eventuality, cruel and unbelievable though it would have been, was always a real possibility.

I think it's fair to say that we fell in love with Burma as we flew over it in preparation to land. So many feelings were caught up in association with this place and it was impossible to know Nicholas Greenwood without being totally absorbed by his affection for the country. It is indeed unspoiled, beautiful, welcoming and unique. Her people are delightful and their whole way of life is fascinating. But first we had to be allowed in.

Having queued for absurd amounts of time both to get in and then to get out of Thailand, I had assumed that getting past Myanmar Immigration Control was going to be a long haul. There were no queues to speak of in the hall; one great mass of bodies, largely South-East Asian, clammered for position, mostly to stay upright. It wasn't until we got close to the desk with which we were sort of in line that we realised it was for diplomats only. Convinced that we would be thrown back onto the first plane leaving our prize destination that evening, I was delighted to set foot beyond passport control with little delay and onto the soil of Myanmar.

Our guide, U Zaw Win, had the kindest, brownest eyes I have ever seen. This man would take me to my uncle for sure, unless we were to be extraordinarily unlucky. We got along with him extremely well and although we respected his main function was to get us to Thanbyuzayat safely, having bribed everyone along the route with the potential to stop us, we also found him a charming travelling companion and we had many a laugh with U Zaw Win.

On arrival in Rangoon I discovered that I had left all of my anti-mosquito preparations in Bangkok. After all the painstaking preparation I had endured, I had committed the worst possible oversight as we headed for Moulmein, swamps and malaria carried by at least one in ten of the mosquito population without precautions. With help from our guide I managed to obtain a sticky gel from a Rangoon stall which was supposed to keep the insects at bay.

Our young driver owned a stall in a local market together with his own mini-bus, which was to be our transport in Rangoon. The tune on the cassette player as we took off for our hotel was 'the Yellow Rose of Texas', which I shall never forget. The same tape included assorted country and western songs about dead cowboys' ghosts wandering the desert, which could have been deemed inappropriate if it hadn't been amusing. To be in Burma at last, to actually *be* there was a great mixture of indescribable feelings but they certainly included excitement, relief and anticipation as well as a little fear.

When you are constantly told that you cannot do something or that you are not allowed to venture somewhere, the inference or even the stated deterrent is one of danger. I could not believe that U Zaw Win was about to lead us into any kind of mortal peril, in fact, the poor man had only just returned from a trip to Thanbyuzayat with a group of assorted tourists, two of them British. However, anticipating trouble made us feel all the more blessed that we were able to avoid it although that may have been more by luck than judgement on a few occasions.

The hotel was potentially well geared up to a flood of tourists, should they ever arrive, and made us very welcome. That evening we were spared the delights of the dining room, where the food, once probably delicious, didn't ever seem to unite with your plate until it was stone cold and had been exposed to flies. U Zaw Win and his boss, the head of Tamarind Travels and Tours, U Win Sein, took us out on the town to the best restaurant we experienced in Burma. It was Chinese.

Sitting opposite the magnificent golden Shwedagon Pagoda while we ate in the open air, soaking up all the flavour of this extraordinary country, all I could focus on was the 22nd; still four days away.

We boarded the train to Martaban at two o'clock in the morning two days later. As previously observed you do not argue with the time at which anything runs in Burma because you are grateful that it is running at all. So we snatched what sleep we could in preparation for a very long journey. Having been picked up by U Zaw Win and his driver, we were duly taken to Rangoon station to strains of more dead cowboys, where the only signs of life were sleeping station staff in little heaps around the ticket office. There we were joined by U Win Sein and his wife who presented U Zaw Win with the most obscene quantity of food and water supplies for our journey. I began to wonder what we were travelling to.

Luck was on our side because the train arrived ahead of schedule and we were allowed to board soon afterwards. Our first class carriage was built circa 1930 and was basic in the extreme. The fans which once cooled its occupants had ceased to work, probably also in the thirties, which must have been about the time they last cleaned the toilets. I was intrigued to see the thick carpet of flies, mostly dead ones, that lay in each of the covered light fittings above. The chairs appeared sumptuous. Deeply sprung, they held the promise of comfort and, very cleverly, they were designed so that you could sit either classroom style with your neighbours or turn them around so that you faced them. In the latter format, facing U Zaw Win and our personal armed guard, who fell asleep before the train departed, we began our great journey. I was tired, thirsty – but put off from drinking by the state of the toilets, concerned that my back would remind me constantly of the length of the journey ahead and happier than I have ever been in my life. My broad grin became ecstatic as the whistle blew and the train left the station. We were really on our way now.

There was so much to see out of the window. Even in the dark there were lit temples and shrines to be admired as we passed by and it became increasingly lighter, or our eyes became used to the darkness, before the dawn came up like thunder as Kipling had correctly observed it to do so. Suddenly there burst before us the most startling array of colours and the sights and sounds of the Burmese countryside. The farmers tended their cattle as if in slow motion, shrouded in mist. People worked the paddy fields, the light and colours changing constantly as we watched, transfixed.

The variety of the scenery in Southern Burma is remarkable and consists of far more than the tropically obvious palm trees you would expect to see. There were scenes which were reminiscent of England, with green, lush rolling hills and a vast assortment of trees and vegetation at this post-monsoon time. The little villages bustled and wherever the train stopped the locals would parade the length of the train with their wares displayed upon their heads. Delicious smelling food wafted by but because of the flies and our inadequate immune systems for the hazards of such treats, we ate only what our tour guides had provided for us.

Our fellow passengers were all Burmese and there were monks among them. Travellers handed down empty drinks cans to the children on the platforms who can sell them, so you don't see any such debris among the litter in their country. The Burmese are not dirty people, they simply lead a different way of life. The overriding smell, which is Burma, emanates from their penchant for dried fish, which is on sale in the open air and a magnet for flies everywhere you go.

During our journey I was aware of some scuffling on the floor and caught out of the corner of my eye enough visual evidence to persuade me to pretend that I was mistaken about what had passed underneath my seat. It was confirmed, unprompted and unwelcomed, by my fellow passengers, that we had at least one rat on board with us.

Great amusement was provided on and off throughout the journey when the 'comfortable' looking chairs turned out to have an aged suspension, completely at odds with that of the train. Much bouncing ensued at intervals where the track had seen better days. The mere thought of repair would not have occurred to anybody, apparently, but we were still pleased we had travelled by train. The only alternative was the road, which for much of the journey ran alongside the track, where it actually still existed. Craters, rocks, rubble and disappearance are the only words I can think of to describe it.

Our armed guard slept peacefully throughout all of this. I asked my husband quietly if he thought he *was* armed, since as all the Burmese men wear longyis (sarongs) it's very hard to tell. Andrew whispered back that he was at least armed with a biro, since we could see one poking out of his shirt pocket. He finally awoke and vanished mysteriously as we pulled into Martaban.

The Burmese who had accompanied our journey and were not first class passengers had travelled either in cattle trucks or on the roof of the train. There was bedlam at the station when we all disembarked and we had to rush to keep together, heading as we were for our first Immigration Office, where our papers for onward transmission would be approved – or not.

The Immigration authorities were friendly and hospitable, though slow, and it was easy then to wonder what all the fuss had been about. It seemed that provided you had received the correct permission, that it was documented, that fees and bribes had been settled and you were courteous, there was no problem whatsoever. Still I wondered if I was really going to Thanbyuzayat via Moulmein.

We could certainly see Moulmein. It was just across the river from Martaban and it looked stunning from the veranda of the Immigration Office, on the other side. The Salween River, which I had imagined to be the deepest blue, was an overwhelming grey and polluted, the chief offender being raw sewage. Since it would have been in an identical state when John last saw it, it reinforced the purpose of my quest to follow his last steps.

When we were finally allowed to go and board the ferry, a terrifying ordeal began for me. I had with me two large cardboard boxes which had travelled first class on the plane whilst I went economy, courtesy of Thai Airways. One contained crosses which were intended for the Thanbyuzayat Cemetery Memorial and the grave of a friend of John. The other contained John's wreath. I would not be parted from these boxes despite numerous gallant offers to relieve me of them, except on the plane and when I had to put them through the X-ray at Heathrow. I heard the baggage checker at the airport utter only one word as an assortment of luggage passed before him on his screen. "Poppies", he had said.

In the mad scramble for the boat which involved hundreds of Burmese and many tons of produce, fruit, vegetables and so on, in huge bundles, I had no alternative but to do as the natives did and carry my large boxes on my head. There simply wasn't room to carry them in either hand and not end up in the water.

Once on board the passengers kept piling on and so did more produce, until our list to port was enough to alarm the most hardened sailor. It was a mixed blessing then when after much jabbering and delay we learned that we were to change vessels – in mid-river, with nothing to hold on to but hope. Stepping from one, flat ferry platform to another, several swaying feet apart, amidst total chaos and flailing arms, still clutching my precious cargo, was the only frightening moment of the trip.

Once we had safely disembarked, a great crowd of Moulmein residents gathered around us while U Zaw Win went to find our driver for this end of the trip. He had come by road. If the Burmese in this neck of the woods had not seen many white people I don't think they had ever seen a blonde woman. It was weird being stared at and they were standing just on the boundary of being obtrusively close. One smile in their direction, however and they all beamed and dispersed. All they want from foreigners is their friendship and as U Zaw Win explained to us, there is great kudos for his people if they can tell their friends that they have made friends with you.

I was very taken with Moulmein. The streets had great character, the temples were beautiful and the views from the high spots were spectacular. It was very green. Also, our hotel was beside the river and Moulmein seemed to me to have the only breeze in Burma.

Unbelievably, Tamarind Tours had had to bribe the Mawlamyine Hotel to accept our business. The rooms were chalets facing the river and after the traumas of a sleepless night, *that* train journey and *that* ferry crossing, a shower and sleep seemed a good idea. At least, that was what Andrew had set his heart on. I was too excited and I wanted to explore and to be alone with my thoughts for a while.

I went down to the water's edge and finally worked out what it was about Moulmein which was unique in my experience. The palm trees were making a noise, an urgent singing as the wind whistled through their graceful leaves. As I sat and looked out across the river at "Shampoo Island", with all the while the wind calling to me through the trees, my skin bristled. Not only was I looking straight at something I knew that John had seen – he was still there. Never had his presence been so strong in any place. He was talking to me through those trees; welcoming me, beckoning me.

When I returned to our room, the power was off as it had been on our arrival. No great surprise. The room was so unbearably hot and airless I really believed that I would be asphyxiated if I lay down in there. I opened the French windows and was surprised to see U Zaw Win and our driver sitting on their terrace with all their chalet doors and windows open. My logic told me that if they weren't being bitten alive then there was no earthly reason why we should appeal to the local mosquitos either. Unlike the native human residents of Moulmein we would hold no special appeal for them. I left open our doors, pulled the curtains and joined Andrew in sleep.

When we awoke I had 22 mosquito bites and a raging headache. There must have been at least 150 of the little monsters in our room, but once the power was restored and the air conditioning worked, all was well. Apart from the reaction of my skin. The trials and tribulations of this trip, such as they were, were all part of an adventure to us and I was so happy to be on my way to John that nothing bothered me in the least. I was certainly not going to make a fuss about anything which was caused by my own stupidity. I also felt a little invincible. As I had assured my mother before we left, John wouldn't allow anything bad to happen to me on this pilgrimage.

It was the 21st of November and tomorrow was our big day. Surely nothing was going to stop us now. After wading through treacle and clambering across marshmallow floors like the ones in dreams when you are trying to board your flight and you've left your passport at home, I was going to John's grave in Thanbyuzayat War Cemetery, tomorrow.

Above: The talking palms of Moulmein. Shampoo Island is opposite.

Below: Moulmein jail.

I must have drifted into breakfast like a purposeful ghost. Entirely ready for what I was about to do, at last I didn't have to wait any longer. My role was one of messenger and I was so proud to be a part of John's special day. Today was for him.

The Superintendent of the Commonwealth War Graves in Burma, whose own cemetery is in Rangoon, is Oscar Dewar. Peter had known him for many years and it's probably because of this that Oscar went to all the trouble of joining us by road for our visit to Thanbyuzayat. I felt it was a special honour for John and we were delighted because he was an extremely nice man with a brilliant command of English and a good sense of humour, which he knew when and when not to use.

So, with Oscar setting off by car we boarded our mini-bus for the most important 40 miles I have ever travelled. Things were still moving in slow motion and just recalling the experience entirely recreates for me the overwhelming feelings of that day.

We drove past Moulmein jail, where John and the other members of the Sumatra Battalion spent one night before arriving themselves at Thanbyuzayat.

When we arrived at our first SLORC[1] office en route, U Zaw Win leapt off the bus brandishing our clearance papers while we watched anxiously. Very quickly, however, it was all smiles and we were back on our way.

Two other SLORC offices later, we were very close to our destination when we arrived at another. Here, U Zaw Win disappeared from view, for an agonisingly long time. When he reappeared he was waving his arms around in a very agitated manner and appeared to be having heated discussions with the officials. My heart stopped. Surely we were not going to be turned away now. After what seemed a very long time U Zaw Win was back on the bus, explaining that they had wanted us to have an entourage of guards. U Zaw Win had insisted that one was enough and he got his own way in the end. Lunch had to be bought for whoever accompanied us!

At the next village the dreamlike quality of all that I saw persuaded me where we were, though no one said a word. And then the tin rest house came in sight; resplendent, unreal. I was in Thanbyuzayat.

The cemetery was closer than I had realised, just through the village and on our left. As we drove past it to a side entrance which took all vehicles to the caretaker's house, I felt every

[1] The State Law and Order Restoration Council (SLORC) is the political arm of the Burmese Army.

Above: The Thanbyuzayat. (The 'tin resthouse').

Below: Thanbyuzayat War Cemetery. Oscar Dewar is on the left, Mr Oni Ward on the right.

inch of skin on my body stand to attention. The beauty of everything I saw and felt on this day was breathtaking.

Thanbyuzayat War Cemetery has no irrigation system and yet Mr Oni Ward, the caretaker and Oscar Dewar's father-in-law, maintains an exquisite garden of rest. If I had died there I would have wanted to lay there forever. Trees threw cooling shadows over parched but nevertheless green grass. Flowering shrubs abound. Trim little hedges form neat borders. It is a kind of paradise and there before us were the graves of 3,771 men, British, Dutch and Australian.

The road which ran past the cemetery was quiet in that despite its importance as a main route for the people of Thanbyuzayat, most of their transport involved bicycles, horses and only the occasional moped. Opposite the cemetery was a wooden school from which the sweet singing of Burmese children wafted over the graves. There was bird song. Nothing else disturbed the mantle of peace which hung graciously over this amazing place.

I had always imagined that we would enter through the main gates and from here I could have walked to John's grave blindfolded, I had looked so often at the grave plan. Because we had come in at the side of the cemetery and now faced down towards the entrance and I was so totally overcome, I was disorientated. But Oscar and Mr Oni Ward who take their responsibilities seriously, wanted in any case to lead me to my uncle, which they did.

Previously open minded about how I would react to John's grave I suppose it was entirely predictable that I should fall to my knees and howl. It was his grave and I was close to him finally. I felt I had the love of his mother, father and brother to pour out to him, as well as my own and the rest of my family.

I knelt there for some time in private, with all the men a suitable distance away, except for Andrew, who quietly joined me just when I needed him most. He too felt all of the things which I have described, and his involvement and deep caring for John as a person and the Burma-Siam Railway as a whole should not be underestimated. On this one issue, above all others, I am able to communicate my innermost feelings to my husband, without any words.

We could have stayed there for a long, long time but as in most aspects of life, no matter how special or important, there were other people to consider and a schedule to adhere to, looming in the wings. We had to be finished and on our way out of Thanbyuzayat by four o'clock because traditionally that is when the shooting begins. Besides, there were things to do.

I took some soil from around John's headstone and placed it in an envelope. Into the impression I placed a cassette tape of music recorded for John and covered it up, hoping Mr Oni Ward's gardeners might not find it. In front of his headstone I placed two wooden eggs, symbolic of those he did not live long enough to eat and a variation on the Buddhist custom of presenting food to their dead. Beside his headstone I placed a wooden cross with a message from my sister together with my own message and a single poppy which my parents had kissed for him. In front of his headstone I laid the wreath. The grave was tastefully bedecked. John could be in no doubt that he is a very loved man. I felt a bizarre assortment of emotions through which happiness at being able to honour John prevailed.

I attached a photograph of John to his wreath having shown it to Oscar and Mr Oni Ward, who don't often see the faces of men whose graves they tend. I also confessed to having the bronze plaque and some glue for fixing it to the marble surround of John's headstone. They had been so kind and so nice to us that I couldn't bring myself to be dishonest with them and attempt to stick it on without their knowledge. They readily agreed to adhering it themselves for which purpose they had a much better adhesive and promised me that it would be done. I left it in position.

Just behind John's grave lay the remains of Frederick Dobson, "Dobbie", a Sumatra Battalion and 250 AMES colleague with a personality, according to John's other mates, much aligned to his own. John, Dobbie and Raymond Frazer would often go swimming together at Changi, in the good times. I lay a poppy cross on Dobbie's grave.

There were also tributes to place for the descendants of other British occupants of the cemetery and photographs to be taken. I laid my other poppy cross at the foot of the memorial because it was for all the men, of all ranks, ages and nationalities, to assure them that they are not forgotten. Not everyone is as lucky as I am and many people who would love to honour their dead would not be in my enviable position to be able to do so. This cross was for all of them.

We returned to John's grave and I was aware that I had no saliva and felt very dizzy. I came close to passing out and wondered fleetingly if I would be staying in this wonderful place after all, before drinking a bottle of water and pulling myself together.

We had to leave the cemetery then but knew we would return before leaving Thanbyuzayat. Our next visit was to a place where no British have set foot since the war, other than to reclaim the bodies of the men along the line for reburial. It was the site of the camp at Kando, two kilometres away.

The road behind us led back to Thanbyuzayat and the road ahead to the Three Pagodas Pass and the border with Thailand, only 67 miles away. The road on which we stood was the Burma end of the Burma-Siam Railway. It was built over the site of the line. Another railway line

134

crosses the road and is the link to Ye which was there at the time of the war. As you faced Thailand, to the right was a large clearing, treeless and with parched rough ground at intervals. The bases of the huts the men occupied when they worked the line. To the left was a monastery, a pagoda and a Japanese memorial to all the dead.

John and his mates were not in this camp but would certainly have passed through it. Dawson Corbett, Hugh Davies' uncle, had died in this camp. A monk appeared clutching a Japanese business card and an old Burmese man joined us. Both of them had been at Kando when the railway was built. They spoke no English but they understood why we were there.

Kando. The line to Ye crosses the road which was the Burma end of the Burma-Siam Railway.

Chapter 3

After the pilgrimage I suppose we could appreciate Burma even more and our minds and time were freed to sightsee and behave like tourists. We visited a market in Moulmein and bought some betel nut cheroots which are made there and nowhere else. It caused some hilarity when I joined U Zaw Win in smoking one.

We stopped the mini-bus outside Moulmein Jail and I got out with my camera and took some photographs. I could see some movement over there and sure enough some officials appeared and so I got back on the bus. A long conversation ensued with U Zaw Win, during which he apologised for stopping in a curfew area unknowingly and assured the officials that I had not taken any pictures. I would never have thought such a sweet man could be such a blatant liar, but I was awfully grateful.

Later, the day after our trip to Thanbyuzayat, U Zaw Win took us to a temple on the hill. Amongst the many buildings there was one with open windows and not a soul about. I was discreetly led to the most magnificent aerial view of Moulmein Jail, the occupants of which could be clearly seen walking crab-like as they were all chained by the ankles. They are mostly political prisoners. The Burmese joke that there are no criminals in their jails.

We began our journey in reverse back to Rangoon at six o'clock the next morning, travelling to Martaban on the car ferry which was much more civilised. We arrived at the Immigration Office much earlier than our train and so we saw a little of the town. An old gentleman from Moulmein stood and stared at us, pleasantly enough, and then turned to U Zaw Win and explained that he'd never seen a foreigner before. We shook his hand.

When the train arrived, two of its passengers, Swiss backpackers, we think, had not obtained permission to travel either to Martaban or beyond. Having travelled upon the train for nine hours as we had done, the poor souls were put straight back on it for another nine to Rangoon. We realised then, if not before, the importance of doing things as the Burmese stipulate. Accepting that travel is not free as in other parts of the world and that whatever system is in operation must be respected, especially in someone else's country.

Back in Rangoon there followed more temples, Burmese karaoke which is not to be recommended, and sad and tearful farewells with U Zaw Win . We didn't want to leave Burma and certainly not to go back to Bangkok. There were consolations, however. The drinking water on tap in the Asia Hotel, a bath and more palatable food.

There was no way though, that this trip was ever going to be a jolly holiday and our return to Thailand heralded the completion of the pilgrimage, as we travelled to Kanchanaburi. This was the week of the bridge on the Kwai Noi, (Kwai means river, so River Kwai is total nonsense) where a son et lumière takes place once a year. Here we had to endure the commercialisation, some may even say exploitation, by the Thais, of an historic event more synonymous with quiet remembrance than with the lewd display they had gone to so much trouble to put on. The bulk of their audience appeared to be Japanese and Kanchanaburi was strewn with their flags.

The event of course appeared to be suitably pro-British and it was very professionally orchestrated. I was ok about it until they played Malcolm Arnold's superb theme tune for the film, 'The Bridge on the River Kwai'. For this (for which Arnold won an Oscar) he yoked together his own counter-melody with Kenneth Alford's 'Colonel Bogey', and included within it the whistling of the men as they marched from camp to camp, hypnotically beginning the sequence barely audibly and then building the volume.

Advertising urged 'must see bridge on river Kwai illuminations' and far worse, 'must see Kanchanaburi war graves'. I felt sick. So many visitors heed their call for action other than relatives or comrades, that the grass has worn out in this cemetery, flanked by two horrendously busy main roads and thick with carbon monoxide. Just inside the main entrance rather than among the rows of graves, what was the grass has had to be covered with plastic matting.

Obviously, it was the comparison with Thanbyuzayat and its peaceful beauty which distracted so much from the impression left upon us by this equally important place. But the contrast was marked. Especially with the attitude of the people, but since the Burmese are being exploited by their own, unelected masters, perhaps they haven't got around to inflicting the same treatment upon their visitors.

When we crossed the bridge on foot in daylight, we were unaware that most of the wooden base was missing, and that chasms of several feet had to be negotiated. Since we both suffer vertigo in some measure, the crossing took a long time. With so many people following on behind and coming towards us, it was impossible to abandon walking. Without a lot of extended hands towards me of assorted nationalities, however, I don't know how I would have made it.

From this highly significant port of call we went on to view the remains of the Thailand end of the Burma-Siam Railway, often, courtesy of Peter, to parts quite unknown to others. He took us to the beautiful Erawan Waterfall, where he told us he got a free shower when on the line, until Asiatics fouled the river above and it started to deliver cholera with its refreshment.

Andrew and I decided to hire a car and driver to take us to the Three Pagodas Pass on the Thai border. This place, the meeting point for the two ends of the line, was too important to miss and the trip only took a day. We didn't know until we got into the car that the manager of the hotel had decided to join us. He returned brandishing a pack of 200 very cheap cigarettes but may well have had another reason for accompanying us. In my dizzy state, it seemed to me, regardless, that everyone was pulling out the stops to make things happen for us.

We had another purpose for making the journey. We missed Burma terribly and we wanted to go back. Even though U Zaw Win wouldn't be there to meet us and the border territory is Karen so the atmosphere should not have been the same, it was. We sat in Burma, 23km from the border which was as far as we were allowed to go, our passports having been taken from us at the border crossing, drinking our Burmese coffee and watching the natives go about their daily business.

At the border, a signpost marked the 'crossing' of the remnants of the line. Another informed me tantalizingly that Thanbyuzayat was just over 60 miles north. I could have been back with John within the hour, passing the site of all the camps he worked, and the one in which he died, en route.

On our way back we stopped and made the descent to 'Hellfire Pass', so named by the Australians who toiled for 12 arduous weeks to blast and cut their way through solid rock, with the Japanese pelting them with debris from above whilst they did so. There was a natural silence about this spot, in common with all segments of the line we went to, which told its own story. The birds sang and the insects chirped and all life went on around. It did not compare to the eerie noiseless environment which dominates the sites of the concentration camps in Germany, where animals have vacated the scene permanently because they can detect evil. But you still felt that the surrounding area had picked up and recorded what it had witnessed and that it was about to play it back to you at any second.

What also struck us about this place, including the hotel manager who had dutifully climbed down with us, was how little reclamation the jungle had made in this or any other section of line we had seen. Only the most spindly, young and tender trees had made a half-hearted attempt to settle themselves with any permanence on the track.

The final momentous part of our pilgrimage was to take the route of the evacuation for the liberated men, on the train, on the actual line, back to Bangkok. It was hot and it was painfully slow. It made Burma Rail seem like Intercity. But it was something I'm pleased to say I've done. I did it for John, really, because he didn't manage to do it for himself.

After a few days 'recovering' in Bangkok it was time to go home. Home; with a host of memories and emotions which I had not the words to express, for a long time for someone trying to write a book.

Burma

Given the distinctive character of their land, it is all the more extraordinary that the people of Burma span such diverse ethnic groups. The Burmese population comprises Burmans, Shan, Arakanese, Karen (themselves consisting of at least 11 different tribes), Kachin and Mon.

Some Burmese are Muslim but the vast majority are Buddhist. The latter has encapsulated in five commandments the same principles of morality for which those in the Christian faith apparently needed spelt out in ten. Namely, to kill no living thing, not to steal another's property, not to commit any sexual crime, not to speak what is untrue and not to drink intoxicating drinks.

They seem a very gentle, unprepossessing race to me, but perhaps I was exceptionally fortunate in the people I encountered. Certainly, they cope admirably with military rule and lack of material wealth, as I saw things, with their general disposition of outward acceptance of their lot and apparent contentment with life. No one appeared to lack a full stomach or a broad smile.

The truth, I am aware, is somewhat different. No one can applaud military rule, which flies in the face of democracy and the will of the people. They are of course suppressed as a result.

Their public transport is unreliable and potentially dangerous in terms of the absence of maintenance and overcrowding. You don't go there for the haute cuisine or for relaxation. Anything from a stomach upset to something much more serious accompanies a visitor from the west, virtually as a prerequisite. Insect bites can cause much more than a swelling. Gross outspokenness in the wrong quarters could lead to very serious trouble indeed. But I absolutely adored the place. I felt at home in Burma and I was prepared to put up with anything.

As Nicholas Greenwood says in his book, 'Guide to Burma', "Burmese trains hurtle along at speeds of up to 30 mph.... Again, just keep smiling: after all, your not on Myanma Airways."

With reference to the latter, he recalls, fondly: "As one UB (Union of Burma Airways) employee expressed when I foolishly inquired what time my flight from Pagan to Mandalay was departing; 'why you ask me? Ask the pilot.'"

My interest in Burma goes beyond the fact that her people are the eternal custodians of my uncle's physical remains.

It is hard to imagine anyone visiting Burma without being fascinated by it, if only because western influence is so negligible and the country appears frozen in time. I certainly haven't visited another place which has retained all its own natural flavour; apparent in every way in Burmese daily life.

The fact that Burma has over 80 different languages explains why Nicholas, conversant in Thai, has not mastered more than basic Burmese, he says, in an inordinate number of trips. He went to Rangoon one day, for the day, for a photograph he'd forgotten to take on a previous trip for his latest travel guide – from England. As he says, the older generation speaks English but few of the younger, as a result of the government's efforts to blot out external influence. It is ironic that this oppression is keeping Burma Burmese.

As he also says, if you are lucky enough to eat Burmese home cooking it is streets ahead of the food commonly served in their restaurants or hotels, but one night U Zaw Win treated us to chicken with rice and vegetables at the hotel in Moulmein, and it was a huge improvement on the nightly omelette and chips which I'd thought was all my upset stomach could contend with. The meat dishes, however, conjure up the words, 'skinny cattle' all over again. All bones and little meat. Burmese chickens look as if they've been shut sideways in a door.

Although this charming tribal race have been left in comparative peace by the rest of the world and nothing mechanical functions as we have come to demand it, they are a highly civilised people. So the women wearing bark powder on their faces, primarily as a protection against the sun, but which has tribal connotations for us, gives them another unique individuality.

When we first met Oscar Dewar, the Superintendent of the Burma War Graves based just outside Rangoon, we were in his cemetery. There are only two in Burma. The Rangoon cemetery contains the graves of men who fought the Japanese in order to win back control of Burma during the war. Oscar was most concerned that some of the bronze plaques on the same, flat headstones as in Thanbyuzayat, were being stolen by local youths. They were breaking into the cemetery at night to steal them and were melting them down to make jewellery to sell.

There were three awful consequences of this. The bronze was being replaced by plastic substitutes by the commission; the cemetery and its visitors were subjected to security arrangements and the rot was apparently setting into Burma just as it is in our own territory, despite their segregation.

I'm sure that this was the reason that we were not able to enter the front gates of Thanbyuzayat, except by request later on. Mr Oni Ward had anticipated problems in this glorious village, long before, if at all, he had any cause for concern.

I find it inappropriate to draw comparisons with rising crime amongst juveniles at home and the youth of Burma, especially in the light of the brutal regime under whose strict rule they have to live. Details of a classic example of this were sent to me by Robert Anderson (my Battalion friend) on the 29th of July 1994.

Villagers who had fled to refugee camps on the Thai-Burmese border described 12 hour days, beatings, horrific accidents and debilitating illness (including malaria and cholera). Worse, they reported that they had received no money and no food.

The Burmese government explains their exploitation of their own people with the assurance that they are patriotic volunteers working in lieu of taxation.

Between 20,000 and 60,000 villagers, together with chain-gangs of prisoners from local jails, are said to be being forced to labour at any one time on the project in monsoon conditions.

The goal of the Burmese government is to complete a railway line from Ye down to Tavoy. Both places are further south of Thanbyuzayat, where we saw the Ye line cross the existing road which was once the Burma-Siam Railway. Its principal purpose is to service a proposed natural gas pipe-line into Thailand from an Andaman Sea field and the junta insists it will help boost living standards in the Tenasserim Division. They are also placing an emphasis on the much needed upgrading of transport facilities in Burma generally.

So the Ye-Tavoy Railway rises like the living dead to haunt us. That it is so close to the site of the Burma-Siam Railway simply adds insult to injury. That history can and does repeat itself and that some lessons are apparently never learned should serve to depress us all. But I will return to Burma. After a revisit to the cemetery I want to explore *that* road. *That* road which stands where the railway lay and follows the length of it all the way to the Three Pagodas Pass. Despite it being even more off-limits than John's resting place, it will remain a burning ambition until I have seen it.

The evacuation route, too, is a journey I will undertake and Mergui and Tavoy are vital ports of call, but although I thought at one time this could be immediate, putting all practical considerations aside, I'm still overwhelmed by Moulmein and Thanbyuzayat. I would not be able to return for a long time.

Chapter 5

Back to the Railway

Rohan D Rivett, who was an Australian war correspondent prisoner of war, manages perfectly to portray the misery of the railway, balanced with its miraculously prevailing spirit, in his book "Behind Bamboo".

He refers to the 55km 'hospital camp', in which John died, as the 'sick dump', which he says was opened in July 1943 by the inauspicious arrival of Colonel Coates, the chief medical officer, on a stretcher. The colonel was, however, suitably nursed back to some semblance of health very quickly, to enable him to carry out his duties.

Although he reiterates the conditions there as previously described, he details the resourcefulness of a Dutch chemist named Boxal, who managed to extract a novocaine solution from the meagre cocaine in Colonel Coates' possession which proved vital in some of the many surgical operations the Colonel had to perform, particularly amputations. He also managed to produce from an extraction of ipecacuanha[1], a precious solution of emetine. There was little of it, but those dysentery sufferers lucky enough to have been treated with it showed an immediate and marked improvement.

The author is unstinting in his praise of all the Australian MOs, as were their patients of all nationalities, for whom they did so much – with so little. Their sincerity inspired men to believe that they would recover, even though the MOs didn't usually have the necessary treatment to administer. They, in turn, acknowledged that some of their best orderlies had had no medical training.

It should also be noted that the Japanese eventually supplied the camp with a spray and pump for the treatment of ulcers with potassium permanganate. Of the 2,400 ill and dying men who occupied the camp not long after its opening, about 800 suffered from tropical ulcers. Many of them developed dysentery and malaria as well, whilst resident in the 'hospital'.

On the subject of a medical incident at Thanbyuzayat, the base camp, also a 'hospital', which was bombed by allies, I quote the author in full because it sums up their general situation so eloquently. The following passage relates to Surgeon-Commander Epstein of the US Navy:

> *"On another occasion, the commander, after inspecting a sick man, turned to the orderly accompanying him and reeled off a prodigious list of drugs and potions to be administered at intervals to the patient; then he moved off towards his quarters. A bewildered orderly came panting after him: "But Sir," he stammered, "we haven't got any one of those drugs you prescribed for ...". "I know," replied the commander grimly, "but if he's going to live, that's what he needs".*

---

[1] A low-growing South American rubiaceous shrub, cephaelis ipecacuanha. The drug prepared from the dried roots of this plant is used as a purgative and emetic.

Conversely, the humour with which this man writes is heart-warming, because you cannot fail to believe that at least the bulk of the prisoners of the Japanese maintained a similar attitude.

He refers to the sick seizing every opportunity for a laugh. Specifically, he recalls an incident when a padre passed the 'hospital' one day, wearing only his shorts. He is talking about one of the bamboo and attap huts which housed the sick, either from dysentery or tropical ulcers or something equally dreadful. From the dark depths of the hut came a voice: "I say, padre, how much did you get for the shirt.".

Even written with typically Australian candour, as it undoubtedly is, I found his book tremendously uplifting. Only a man who was there has the right to laugh at any aspect of the railway, but through his book, he has shared this opportunity with others.

It helps to add a modicum of sanity to the proceedings, and underlines the fact that in order to win through, men simply had to make the best of their lot and get on with it. It shouldn't have been that way, but it was, and it brought an inordinate number of men back home.

Chapter 6

Home

It must have been both weird and wonderful for prisoners who survived, were liberated and found themselves back in the normal world.

They were fattened up a bit on their journey home, but they had to adjust gradually to having nutritious, varied food in larger quantities. The services kept the men amply supplied with bars of chocolate and cigarettes, too.

An Australian described how although he had dreamt of roast beef and chocolate sauce for three and a half years, and towards the end of his captivity the chocolate sauce was on his roast beef, he could only eat bread and butter for a long while. It's still his favourite food.

Many ex-FEPOWs, understandably, cannot abide the waste of food and they are a joy to cook for. I'm sure I'm not the only one that conspires to give them extra helpings, and yet these great gentlemen retain, to all outward appearances, a healthy physique and sound state of mind.

Appetites went the other way with some, who are completely unable to stomach a large meal in one sitting. They prefer to snack and perhaps without a determined Mrs ex-FEPOW on hand to administer the nutrients, would have faded away long ago.

There were of course returning prisoners who found they had been written-off and replaced by their partners when they came back. It was heartbreaking. There are others who returned to resume rudely interrupted marriages or relationships, who along with their spouses, had enormous adjustments to make. They really had to start again from scratch.

I know that Charles Peall will forgive me for naming him in conjunction with a very touching 'welcome back, dear' story. Because soap on the Burma-Siam Railway was such a rare commodity and it was barely seen by the men for so many years, he had collected every scrap of it which he encountered on his way home and put it in his kit bag. He must have created something of a genuine shortage of the stuff wherever he went. Charles and Wendy have been devotedly married for many years, but it didn't get them off to a very good start on Charles' return when he dumped his prize, waxy booty onto their highly polished dining table.

What I've written will inevitably be read by my heroes, one-time prisoners of the Japanese, and they will judge me. I feel uncomfortable about voicing opinions on a subject better known to them than to me. But I have found it absorbing to find out about their story; my respectful fascination with it has driven me to discover all I can about it. It is actually impossible to become that involved without forming opinions. For instance, it seems to me that the incidence of arthritis in ex-FEPOWs is inordinately high and beyond coincidence. That it is very likely that overwork and malnutrition in constant humidity, let alone stair-rod rain, has greatly increased the chances of developing this particular malaise in men who worked the line.

I have never met an ex-prisoner who complained of anything very much, and certainly not ill health as a result of their treatment. But digestive and many other more serious disorders abound, and I know polite restraint when I see it.

Just as everybody found their own way to deal with their sorry situation on the railway, they have found their own way to cope with the aftermath. As soon as I began my research I realised that there are an enormous number of people whose lives have been touched in some way by it. Many of them are contemporaries. We are everywhere. People I barely know have surviving uncles who will not talk about their experiences under any circumstances. I doubt that there are many men who do not still keep in contact with a mate or two, however.

Joe White, Jim Hall and Bob Bush have kept in touch. Sadly, Joe lost touch with Harry Strike, who has assumed celebrity proportions for me, since Arthur Hargest first mentioned him to me as a contact for information on John and Joe has shown me his photograph. But they had not discussed their collective memories until they found themselves in the company of my father and myself. They had talked about anything and everything – except that.

Peter Dunstan, upon retirement, flung himself headlong into intensive work tracking graves and stories of deaths. I can imagine how dreadful it must be for those who lost relatives and don't know what happened to them, or where they lie.

Charles Peall also dedicates horrendous hours for no financial remuneration in order to keep ex-comrades together through numerous associations and clubs. More than that, he is a vital link with the media and their contemporary portrayal of part of British history which has been hitherto neglected.

And why is this? Why should British servicemen who suffered alongside our allies be virtually ignored? Embarrassment springs to mind. Red faces in Whitehall. The men received their back pay and a pat on the head and were virtually told to get on with it. Their 'compensation' was an insult.

It is said that the first casualty of war is the truth. Despite our freedom, for which cause so many gave their lives in World War Two, we are subjected to propaganda in our democracy. It was vital to the war effort that morale was kept at its peak, and the shame of defeat in the Far East was not allowed to overshadow the gains made against Germany. Quite frankly, the handling of our conflict with Japan was an abortion. The returning prisoners, who were our own hostages of war, bungled in this case, were swept as swiftly as possible under the national carpet.

Many men had recurrent nightmares. I'm sure that some still do. There was no recognition of post traumatic stress disorder in 1945; it hadn't been invented. If ever there was cause to do so, however, it was in the treatment of these victims. Ex-FEPOWs are frequently asked to be source material for the psychologists, whose professional opinions aid lawyers in the settlement of huge compensation claims for modern day sufferers of often brief encounters with conflict around the world. Despite one's temptation to ask what the FEPOW has taught them about the job, the medical profession has extracted from them, details of memories they have not even revealed to their own wives.

Sometimes it seems that the burden of guilt for the lost men who never made it home is borne on the shoulders of the survivors who did. It's as if they took up the mantle because nobody else did, and I know that they remember their comrades. I hope that surviving lives have not been ruined, but I'm also sure that some have.

146

"When you take a life and steal its shadow, all that's left is humanity. When you take a man and steal tomorrow, all that's left is you and me." Black Sabbath 1994

It was five months after my return from Burma before I could continue to write. Although my family had every right to be pleased for me and to assume that I had achieved what I set out to do and had therefore experienced some sort of liberation, I was inordinately depressed and confused.

I really did feel that I had been floating around the Far East in some sort of dream as opposed to really being there, and retrospectively it appears even more unreal than it did at the time. It all seemed very inconclusive to me and my feelings were further frustrated by my inability to 'resurrect' my uncle. What had I really achieved when the outcome remained unaltered and John lay dead in Thanbyuzayat?

It was an equally long time before I could discuss this with my parents. I had effectively come to terms with everything before I could confide any of my previous frustrations. As always, my mother voiced extraordinary empathy when she said that she knew my pilgrimage would be an anti-climax in a sense because of my apparent conviction that I was going to John as if I was going to meet him.

This was not a literal notion. It was never an assumption nor a delusion in any conscious way. I really did go to Thanbyuzayat with an open mind, not knowing how I would react. I pictured nothing in my mind beforehand except kneeling at his grave, apart from a recognised fantasy; that I would see him in the garden. I did not. If John was in that cemetery he walked in with me.

The journey to Burma signified many things. That it defied the bureaucracy that had contrived to keep me out was not the least of the gains made. That I had been able to pay my respects to the dead and living victims of the Burma-Siam Railway was no mean feat. That John was shown with actions how much he is still loved was not unsatisfactory. The past, however, remained stubbornly unmoved.

The five month delay between experiencing the most extreme emotions and transcribing them proved essential and were put to good use. I realised during this interlude that what I had endured was a bereavement. A belated, self-inflicted, somewhat removed bereavement, but a real one nonetheless. I had entered it in despair and anger, but had finally emerged triumphant, much the wiser and at relative peace. It was a revelation to me. It was also Easter 1995.

There is much controversy in the Christian faith about the true meaning of the resurrection of Jesus Christ. This has always been futile and seems, to me, to miss the point. Whether his resurrection was literally the bringing back to life of a corpse or spiritual rebirth is surely irrelevant. The message is hope. The message is that death is not the end.

Eventually, I did feel a sense of fulfilment. I mourned my uncle's loss and will forever continue to do so, but now with a gentle acceptance. I no longer wrestled with a torturous desire to achieve impossible things like changing the course of history or bringing back the dead. With his fate and his loss acknowledged properly I could revere his short life and his memory, uncomplicated by other clutter in my mind. He did live once. He was a part of our world, and nor can that fact be altered.

148

"I can't light no more of your darkness. All my pictures seem to fade to black and white." Elton John 1974

When I found myself swept up in my preoccupation to construct an identikit picture of my uncle and his personality in order to appreciate him fully, I guarded fiercely against the obvious danger of turning him into just what I wanted him to be. Mindful of a child's classic fantasy which creates the perfect, imaginary playmate and of the shortcomings in everyone we know which necessitates compromise in all our relationships, I successfully resisted imagining John as a perfect human being.

I remain convinced, though, that we would have got along very well.

John, like me, was born in the year of the dragon. The Chinese consider all those born under this powerful sign to be special. They are said to hold great promise of success and achievement.

It is highly significant that Arthur Hargest felt that John would be closer to other colleagues with whom he worked. In fact, Arthur saw more of the real John than anyone else that I've had the pleasure to meet from his service days. The fact that John is remembered as having been gentle and quietly spoken is something else which his family can be proud of, but I believe that John would have had plenty to say had he felt it appropriate to express himself.

Although I'm grateful that I found the inspiration to write this account and had the opportunity to do so, it has been a painful experience. It's as if sometimes the words were wrenched out of me instead of just flowing on to the paper. When I handed my father the first two parts for him to read I waited anxiously for his reaction. My mother had told me that although he gave his permission for my research, which I had expressly asked for, he was actually very uncertain about the wisdom of my actions. Perhaps more pertinently, he was distressed about what I might discover.

Although I had revealed some of the contents of John's story, bit by bit to prepare him for the final outcome, much of it was unknown to him when he sat down to read it.

His reaction was to tell me that he had been unable to stop reading it until he finished it, and that upon finishing it he had cried. When I expressed my deep concern for this, because it had never been my wish to upset him with my account of John's life, he said that he was glad that he had been able to cry for the first time for the loss of his brother, in over 50 years.

When Nicholas Greenwood edited this book, he commented that I had not minced my words; that my bitterness towards the Japanese was obvious. I was genuinely surprised at his reaction, because I had begun my research relatively objectively, without enough initial knowledge to be overloaded with prejudice. My discoveries gave everyone in John's family the chance to breath a welcome sigh of relief. The story I uncovered may not have exonerated the Japanese but it certainly placed things in a better overall perspective.

What I discovered about the Japanese and their treatment of John and his fellow prisoners angered me greatly, but I also found that I had to come to terms with the apparent and unexplained desertion of John and 250 AMES by the RAF. I had then to learn to live with the almost unbelievable failure of the defence of Singapore, which led to their captivity in the first place.

Percival conceded full responsibility for the fall of Singapore on his deathbed, but that just compounds my sadness. In a way, the fact that he was prepared to take all of the responsibility upon himself only goes to prove that it wasn't all his fault. No one person could possibly be entirely responsible anyway, for a series of actions involving other command from beneath as well as from above.

Captain Apthorp acted in the very best interests of his men by transferring his sick to the 'hospital' camps on the line and he in turn was under the overall command of Brigadier Varley at the time. But I have to ask myself why my uncle still had eggs underneath his 'pillow' when he died. Raymond Frazer put forward a most reasonable explanation. In a camp full of sick and dying men, was there anyone available to cook John's eggs for him?

Raymond Frazer was of course John's fellow 250 AMES member at Khonkhan, and he was also batman to Colonel Coates. Perhaps because of this latter role, he was the only man at the 55km camp to have been acknowledged by the Japanese as suffering from amoebic dysentery. He was present at John's burial. He has also given me his valued opinion that John died of amoebic dysentery, in conjunction with systematic starvation.

The dropping of atomic bombs devastated Japan. It cost lives to save lives. It stopped the war – quickly – and prevented further atrocities and confrontation. But I believe it was an act of aggression which has preoccupied the Japanese conception of World War Two for the last 50 years.

In her nationalistic pride, which is not dissimilar to our own, she found justification to bury her initiation of conflict and defeat in her indignation because of those bombs. Perhaps if we could only find a way to accept this, some mutual acknowledgement and discourse might follow. This has to be better than nothing, since they cannot take back what they did any more than America can retract her bombs.

My dearest Uncle John,

Now that I have found out more about you and some of what happened to you in your life, I feel that I have got to know you. I also feel better qualified to regard you as the friend I've always perceived you to be.

Your life was cruelly forestalled and you've been denied so many years. We've also been robbed of having you in our own lives, which we will always regret with great sadness. But not only did you live your short life to the full, you left a lasting, real impression upon descendants you didn't even get to meet. This is an achievement so rare and forceful, it reflects the importance of your 27 years, your worth as a human being and the love for you of your only living relative who knew you personally – your brother.

I hope that somehow, our regard for you, which is so strong, has got through to you. That you can be aware of the extent of your loss on others.

There was a time, between my visit to your grave and my writing of this letter, in which I thought that you had left me. But then I finally began to realise what you were saying to me and it made me very happy. It seemed to me that since you loved life and yet yours was taken away from you, the best way in which I could merit my pride in being your niece was to live my own life to the full; that I should turn away from my preoccupation of sorrow, just as you would have done if you'd had the chance. I promise I won't let you down.

On your birthday, I shall always have flowers in my home. Christmas will always be accompanied by my remembrance of the day you died. The anniversary of VJ Day, a day you never saw dawn, will always make me think of you. You will figure in my thoughts, because you've changed my life. But they will be positive thoughts.

I held out my hand to you across boundaries which the living cannot fully understand. Perhaps one day you will hold out your hand to me, and when that time comes, I shall take it with joy, and without any fear.

JOHN EDWIN DAVEY

28/10/1916 – 27/12/1943

Loved with a love beyond all telling. Missed with a grief beyond all tears.

Honoured with our hearts, beyond words.

Index

Acknowledgements

This book could simply not have been written without the co-operation of a great many other people. Their actions and contributions, given so freely, and their blind faith in me, have touched me every bit as much as the subject matter itself.

Firstly I must thank Charles Peall, for his love and friendship above all else, but also for suggesting that I keep a few notes on my findings and for impressing upon me the importance of logging dates. Charles had expected that I would produce a few sheets of references and, for a while, so did I. This book is the result of his sound advice. Without his guidance on how to find information among ex-Far East Prisoners of War, I'm quite sure I would not have got this far. The loan of his books and films, personalised in his recounting of his own experiences on the railway, have contributed immeasurably to my understanding of the Burma-Siam Railway and its aftermath. The sweetness of his persuasion also ensured that I wouldn't give up.

Peter Dunstan spent a great deal of his time corresponding with me, and also lent me books and provided a wealth of information. I have Peter to thank for the map of the line reproduced here, which I believe is more accurate than many others. He also accompanied us on our pilgrimage and showed us places we would never otherwise have seen.

I thank my father for his love and bravery. He would not have considered forbidding me to conduct my research despite his fear of what I may find out. The experience of co-writing with him was a great joy to me, and for his invaluable contribution of a vital chapter of this book I am indebted.

Arthur Hargest welcomed me into his home without knowing anything about me, other than that I am John Davey's niece. If he hadn't responded to my Servicepals message, this book would have been much the poorer. He showed me great kindness and the ultimate reassurance that John lives on through others' memories, and Arthur, they were very crucial memories.

Bob Bush, Jim Hall and Joe White gave both my father and I a wonderful opportunity to relive John's final years through their own memories and experiences. The help and support they have given to me is quite remarkable and has enabled me to write with some authority on events which no other published book contains. Jim Hall in particular, through lending me his books on the subject of the railway, embellished with his own copious margin notes, has given me an insight into the real experiences of the men themselves.

Raymond Frazer corresponded with me without having met me. His candidness was particularly valuable in enabling me to write with conviction about John's illness and his death.

He also was very fond of John and the genuine warmth with which he recalled his friend was appreciated by John's family.

"Don't worry, I'll get you to Thanbyuzayat" said Nicholas Greenwood, and he did. He is an immensely modest man who will cringe when he reads my words of praise, but it goes without saying how much I owe to Nicholas, when everybody else said that I would not be allowed to go. He too gave unstintingly of his time, not only to ensure that I fulfilled my pilgrimage in safety, but that I was able to appreciate the wonder of Burma and her intensely lovable people whilst I was there.

For his most sympathetic editing of my manuscript. I am eternally grateful.

I am also particularly grateful to Robert Anderson, an Army Sergeant who was a member of the British Sumatra Battalion but who didn't know John. This kind gentleman has telephoned me and has given me all manner of information, including press cuttings on pertinent books, together with details of the current political situation in Burma. He also sent me a colour plate of Chalker's drawing of the 55km camp, Khonkhan, in which John died. Something which he had taken from his own personal files in order to give to me. A gift which I shall treasure.

Tom Watson inspired me through his letters. Because he lost his father during World War Two and as a fellow researcher covering the same period of history, I found his tips and ideas to be very helpful. He also introduced me to Peter Dunstan, and Jack Cosford and his book, 'Line of lost lives'.

My husband's patience and support were of vital importance to me but I thank him most of all for his empathy, which I know came straight from his heart.

I thank Denise Stevens for typing the manuscript, in all its various stages of development and version, and for her critical eye and spell-check which were so necessary for publication.

Lastly, I wish to thank David Plumb, my designer and friend for many years, for presenting my words so beautifully, for his constant reassurance and deep involvement in the production of this book.

The author applauds the music industry and artistes whose haunting melodies are so often accompanied by memorable lyrics.

Those lyrics used as chapter headings, in order of their appearance, are reproduced with kind permission and are credited as follows:

158

Of the many books utilised for research purposes, the following are quoted from with kind permission of the publishers:

The British Sumatra Battalion Ann Apthorp
Published by The Book Guild

Behind Bamboo Rohan D Rivett
The War Diaries of Weary Dunlop E E Dunlop
Published by Penguin Books Australia Limited

Japan at War Haruko Taya Cook & Theodore F Cook
Published by New Press